Adult Learning
and the Challenges
of the Twenty-First Century

Adult Learning
and the Challenges
of theTwenty-First Century

©AWE, Association for World Education

Printed in Denmark by Jelling Bogtrykkeri Ltd.
June 1997

Cover by Svend Hansen

ISBN 87-7838-278-5

Distribution:
Odense University Press
Campusvej 55
DK - 5230 Odense
Denmark
Ph. 0045 66 15 79 99
Fax 0045 66 15 81 26
E-mail: Press@forlag.ou.dk
WWW-Location: http://www.ou.dk/press

Adult Learning
and the Challenges
of the Twenty-First Century

Edited by Ove Korsgaard

Association for World Education

Contents

Ove Korsgaard
Preface 6
Introduction 10

I. ADULT LEARNING, DEMOCRACY, AND DEVELOPMENT

Shirley Walters 16
Democracy, Development & Adult Education in South Africa
Dani W. Nabudere 28
Adult Learning, Human Rights and Democracy in Africa
Holger Bernt Hansen 47
Adult Learning, Democracy and Danish Development Assistance

II. ADULT LEARNING, CHANGING CONFIGURATIONS AND CIVIL SOCIETY

Jorge Jeria 61
Globalization, Internationalization, Regionalization:
A Challenge for Adult Education
Michael Welton 67
Repair, Defend, Invent:
Civil Societarian Adult Education faces the Twenty-First Century
Judit Ronai 76
Adult Education and the Hungarian and Central-European Situation
Hanne Petersen 84
Changes in the Global Judicial Conception

III. ADULT LEARNING, FOLK IDENTITY AND WORLD EDUCATION

Henning Eichberg 88
Otherness in Encounter. Thinking Folk Identity.
Democracy and Civil Society with the Help of Martin Buber
Mabud Fatema Kabir 100
A Philosophy for World Education

Edicio dela Torre 106
What is the Link between Education for Life and World Education?

IV. CONCERNING THE DISCUSSION
ABOUT THEME ONE IN HAMBURG

Ove Korsgaard.. 113
Adult Learning between Global Economy and National Democracy

Dani W Nabudere 126
AWE statement about Theme One

THE AUTHORS 132

THE ASSOCIATION FOR WORLD EDUCATION 136

Preface

Adult Learning and the Challenges of the 21st Century is the title of Theme One at the Fifth UNESCO Conference on Adult Education in Hamburg, Germany, July 1997. The four previous UNESCO conferences on adult education were held in Helsingør (Elsinore), Denmark, 1949, in Montreal, Canada, 1960, in Tokyo, Japan, 1972, and in Paris, France, 1985.

UNESCO has described Theme One at the conference in Hamburg 1997 as follows:

The social issues and global risks facing today's societies are calling upon the participation and the creativity and competence of all citizens. A learning society is becoming a condition of an active civil society. Forward-looking strategies relying on adult learning are required to meet the democratic aspirations, to foster a culture of peace and to profit from the dividends of peace, to cultivate active and informed citizenships, to build identities, to face the globalization of economies, to deal with ecological threats, to revitalise the north-south cooperation in the context of growing economic, technological and educational gaps:

– *Adult Learning for democracy and human rights*
– *Promoting a culture of peace*
– *Encouraging active citizenship*
– *The role of NGOs*
– *Poverty alleviation*
– *Adult learning and gender issues*
– *Cultural diversity/minority issues*
– *Indigenous peoples*

The Association for World Education was asked by UNESCO to be responsible for Theme One. In AWE we were very pleased to be asked and felt it a great honour to be entrusted with this important assignment.

In different ways the AWE has worked with this theme throughout the last two years.

AWE Seminars and Conferences

In cooperation with the Danish and Hungarian Chapter the AWE has arranged two international seminars and one Nordic conference concerning Theme One:

Gerlev, Denmark 28-30 August 1996
Sopron, Hungary, 1-4 September 1996
København (Copenhagen), Denmark, 22 April 1997

AWE Participation in Regional Preparatory Conferences

AWE members have participated in the following regional preparatory conferences:

Edicio dela Torre, the Philippines, and Kazi Fazlur, Bangladesh took part in the Asian and Pacific Region Conference in Jomtien, Thailand, 16-18 September 1996.

Kachi Ozumba, Nigeria, took part in the African Conference in Dakar, Senegal, 14-18 October 1996.

Judit Rónai, Hungary, Jakob Erle and Ove Korsgaard, Denmark, took part in the European and North American Conference in Barcelona, Spain, 12-14 December 1996.

Teresa Quiroz, Chile, and Ove Korsgaard, Denmark, took part in the Latin American and Caribbean Conference in Brasilia, Brazil, 22-24 January 1997.

Consultative Committee

On behalf of the AWE, Ove Korsgaard has been appointed member of the Consultative Committee established by UNESCO to assist, before and during the conference, in building a consensus on a final version of the two documents: the *Declaration* and of the *Agenda for the Future*.

Journal of World Education

During the last two years the AWE has had a continual discussion about Theme One in the Journal of World Education. Dani Nabudere, Uganda, has edited one issue, Edicio dela Torre, the Philippines, has edited another, and Erik Høgsbro Holm, Denmark, has edited four issues.

Conference Book Published by UNESCO

The AWE has contributed to the Conference Book with an article written by Ove Korsgaard, Denmark, and an AWE statement about Theme One, edited by Dani Nabudere.

Workshops at the Conference in Hamburg

The AWE has prepared two workshops for the conference in Hamburg. Ove Korsgaard will be the monitor of a workshop about "Adult Learning and the Challenges of the Twenty-First Century", and Jakob Erle the monitor of "Pedagogical Challenges promoting Democracy and Culture of Peace".

AWE Publication about Adult Learning and the Challenges of the 21st Century

This publication is based upon lectures given at the various AWE seminars and conferences or articles published in the Journal of World Education during the last two years. Both at the regional UNESCO conferences and at the AWE seminars leading up to Hamburg, globalisation has been a key word. This word has not been used at the four previous world conferences about adult education. The implementation of it, up to the fifth international conference, indicates that adult education is now being confronted with new issues which are best integrated using the concept of globalisation. In this book you will find articles discussing different aspects of globalisation within adult education.

This book does not try to cover all aspects of the connection between adult education, democracy, citizenship, civil society, empowerment and peace. Based on the last two years' discussion in the Association for World Education it looks first and foremost at new aspects caused by globalisation.

Acknowledgements

I should like to express my warm appreciation to the authors of the articles in this book.

Further I wish to thank the Danish Royal Ministry of Foreign Affairs and the Danish Ministry of Education for economic support to the above described activities.

I am very grateful to Inger Højlund, the AWE's International Coordinator, for her great commitment to the assignment of preparing and understanding the theme in Hamburg. Likewise, I want to thank Anna Marie Andersen for valuable help in publishing this book.

Finally, I want to express my sincerest thanks for inspiring cooperation with Paul Bélanger, Director, and Marc-Laurent Hazomé, the UNESCO Institute for Education.

Ove Korsgaard, President AWE
June 1997

Introduction

Ove Korsgaard

INTERNATIONALISATION AND GLOBALISATION

Globalisation – a New Word

"When the rhythm of the drumbeat changes, the corresponding dancing steps also change". So tells an African proverb. The word globalisation indicates that the rhythm of the drumbeat is changing. At all the regional UNESCO conferences, leading up to Hamburg, globalisation has been a key word. A quotation from the African declaration, made at the regional conference in Dakar 1996, summarises the general trend: "The globalisation of exchanges and the resulting interdependence, like the competition for acquisition of the excellence that it engenders, nurture the prodigious development of science and technology and make knowledge and intelligence the materials and tools at the same time"[1].

The word globalisation has not been used at the four previous conferences about adult education. Why, then, has it been implemented up to the fifth international conference? Is it that globalisation has become a fashionable word? Or is it that adult education is now being confronted with new issues which are best integrated using the concept of globalisation?

Internationalisation and Globalisation

There is an important difference between the two concepts: international and global. Historically and conceptually the word international is connected with the word national and is based on the assumption that the decisive actors on the international scene are stable national states. For example the UN and UNESCO are founded on the fact that it is the national states which are the legitimate foundation of these institutions.

On the other hand, the word global is not counterpoised in the same way but is connected to the word local. The global and the local are mutually deeply connected which is expressed in the slogan "Think global – act local" and "Think local – act global".

We may distinguish between an increased internationalisation of economic intercourse, and the emergence of a qualitatively new global economy. The world-wide international economy is one in which the principal entities are nation-states; it involves the growing inter-connection between national economies. Interconnections are of the "billiard ball" type; international events do not directly penetrate and permeate the domestic economy, but are reflected through national policies.

Economic globalisation, on the other hand, involves qualitative change towards a system into which distinct national economies are subsumed and re-articulated, essentially by international processes and transactions. The international system becomes autonomised as markets and production become truly global. Whereas intensified economic interdependence involves more of the same in the sense that economic intercourse between national economies increases, true economic globalisation invokes a qualitative shift toward a global economic system that is no longer based on autonomous national economies but on a consolidated global marketplace for production, distribution and consumption. Here the global economy dominates the national economies existing within it[2].

Information Technology and Globalisation

In very uneven ways, trends towards globalisation are transforming finance, currency, trade, employment, social systems, communication, modes of living, the formation of societies, the deep-rooted structures underlying national societies, governance patterns – and adult education and training. Particularly the progress af information technology seems to be a decisive force behind globalisation. As a result of extensive technical investment the cost of storing a given unit of information, of processing it, and of transmitting it over intercontinental distances has declined by factors of a million to one hundred million – efficiency gains that appears to be the most radical in all of economic history to date. The inherent capacity for handling massive amounts of information is both enabling and requiring global economic activities to be organised on a global scale. The process is breaking down the barriers between national economies, diluting their separate identities and inducing unusually rapid shifts in their internal patterns of employment. It is differently affecting men and women, the rich and the poor, the industialised and less industrialised.

In the global market-economy the importance of world trade continues to grow, multinational companies whose turn-over often exceeds the economic resources of small domestic economies are gearing themselves to global business strategies; on the international money markets, hundreds of billions of dollars are traded every day, only a fraction of which goes into trade in commodities. Financially speaking there is already: ONE WORLD[3].

The global "flow" of capital weakens the possibilities of the nation-state carrying out an economic policy based on national premises. Increasingly, national governments are unable to control the international capital which, with supersonic speed, crosses the borders. To compensate for this loss of political capability, new international institutions have been created in order to regulate and coordinate economic policy, for example the World Trade Organisation, the International Monetary Fund, the World Bank, Organisation of Petroleum Exporting Countries and the European Union.

But at the same time as regional economic blocks and regional integrative mechanisms are being worked out, regional, national and ethnical differentiation and tensions are reappearing. The rapid expansion of communication and transport is not only making a global economy, it is also breaking down traditional economic and social structures.

Skyscrapers and Shantytowns

Globalisation has redrawn the world economic map. New centres of vigorous growth based on world trade have emerged in the Pacific rim. On the other hand, whole regions are being economically and politically marginalised. Globalisation is clearly an uneven process, accompanied by fragmentation and marginalisation.

The majority of women and men in the world do not participate in the industrial heartland af nations and regions. Many of them subsist in a "shantytown-economy" in the shadows of the cities.

Fragmentation and marginalisation is also beginning to make an appearance in the wealthy industrial countries. Under the process of international competition social policies and employment protection regulations are being cut back, the number of the unemployed and the "working-poor" is increasing.
Globalisation tends to break down the division of the world into North, South, East, and West, and instead produce a dual-economic system all over the world. Each nation, each region, and the world in general consists of skyscrapers and shantytowns, existing side by side. They are not separate and exclusive ways of life, but integrally bound up with one another, different

manifestations of an integral reality: a global skyscraper and shantytown economy[4].

Population Growth

In the age of globalisation another phenomenon is occurring of comparable magnitude and significance. The demographic momentum that already has been established will produce a historically unique surge over the next decades. It took all of human history up to 1800 to reach the level of one billion people and roughly 125 years to add the second billion. According to some estimates, there will be at least 8,7 billion people alive in 2025, compared with 5 billion today.

It is evident that there is a tension between the economic globalisation and population growth. So far at least, economic globalisation has first of all produced wealth in the Western industrial societies. In these societies the population is stationary or may decline, while for example Kenya's population will be three times today´s in 2025. It is difficult to imagine that social coherence should be preserved decade after decade with economic growth occurring at the top of the prosperity pyramid and population growth at the bottom. Those societies that do not produce a more equitable pattern of development will be in serious trouble, and the world as a whole will be very insecure if too many of its societies fail to achieve basic standards of equity[5].

Sustainable Development

The challenge for the twenty-first century is to find the way between Rio and Copenhagen, between the environment and social development, between the Earth Summit and the Social Summit.

At the World Summit on Social Development, held in Copenhagen, Denmark, 1995, it was for the very first time in history decided to eradicate poverty. The Summit made a political, ethical, social, and even an economic statement: it is now an imperative of humankind to eradicate poverty.

The economic demands of this fundamental requirement are impressive. A more equal distribution of the prosperity in the world is without any doubt necessary, but simple redistribution policies do not give an acceptable outcome. There are too few rich and too many poor for any feasible amount of generosity in the form of income or wealth transfers to be the basic answer. Adequate standards of equity will have to be achieved through broadly distributed growth.

But at the same time the World Summit on Environment and Development, held in Rio 1992, made it clear, that it is necessary to change the forces that are moving the world towards the destruction of the natural resources of our planet. Unlimited material growth will not only produce a still greater deterioration in global ecology, sufficient resources simply do not exist for the world's population to adopt ways of life comparable to those of the First World societies. Ecological problems highlight the new and accelerating interdependence of global systems and bring home to everyone the depth of the connection between personal activity and planetary problems.

The problems of the environment are different for the rich and the poor, for men and for women. The high income countries reduce sustainability by their unrestrained demand for an even higher production of resource-intensive, polluting character, with the accompanying damage that this causes. In poor countries, the demand for food and fuel is rapidly growing and poor population leads to deforestation, soil erosion, silting, and depletion of water supplies. The poor not only contribute to local environmental degradation, but also suffer most from it[6].

Certainly, in the poor countries women are most affected by environment degradation. Therefore, the link between women's empowerment and the development of new values in relation to the environment is critical. There is a strong argument for women to be placed at the centre of development in the twenty-first century. Another key to the next century seems to be a radical change of lifestyle in the developed countries. A de-emphasis on continual economic accumulation will almost certainly be necessary if the ecological risks we are facing now are to be minimised[7]. The ecological risks place mankind in a new form of togetherness. It will not extinguish the conflict between rich and poor but define it in a new way, based on the global limit as a common denominator.

As Jacques Delors says in *Learning: The treasure within*, "The truth is that all-out economic growth can no longer be viewed as the ideal way of reconciling material progress with equity, respect for the human condition and respect for the natural assets that we have a duty to hand on in good condition to future generations"[8].

Seen in this light it can be concluded that the fundamental interest of adult learning is none other than the future of humankind itself.

Notes:

1. "Declaration on Adult Education and Life-long Learning". From the regional UNESCO conference in Dakar, Senegal, 14-18 October 1996
2. Hans-Henrik Holm and Georg Sorensen: *Whose World Order? Uneven Globalization and the End of the Cold War*, Westview Press, 1995
3. John D. Steinbruner: *"Global Economic Power and Cultural Dominance: Where does the West's Power End?"* From af speech made at the Development and Peace Foundation Symposium on The Politicization of Culture, held 9-10 December 1996, Düsseldorf, Germany
4. Shirly Walters (ed.): *Globalization – Rethinking Adult Education and Training: Impacts and Issues*, ZED Books 1997
5. John D. Steinbruner: *"Global Economic Power and Cultural Dominance: Where does the West's Power End?"*
6. *Our Creative Diversity. Report of the World Commission on Culture and Development*. UNESCO Publishing 1995
7. Anthony Giddens: *"Modernity and Self-Identity. Self and Society in the Late Modern Age"*. Polity Press, Cambridge 1991
8. *Learing: The Treasure Within. Report to UNESCO of the International Commission on Education for the Twenty-First Century*, UNESCO Publishing 1996.

Democracy, Development and Adult Education in South Africa

Shirley Walters

INTRODUCTION

South Africa is in a transition to democracy from an authoritarian, colonialist, and apartheid past. It has been held up as one of the beacons of light in a world of the dog-eat-dog realities of globalized capitalism. A key question for adult educators and trainers in the country is what should they be doing in order to enhance the possibilities for a more people-centred social and economic programme of transformation to succeed in South Africa at a political moment when global economies dictate neoliberal market-based policies as the only acceptable solutions? The assumption is made that it is only through a radical transformation which seeks "alternative development" which foregrounds human development, as elaborated by the South-based women's network DAWN[1], that the position of the majority of women will change for the better.

Within this view, a gender perspective is crucial which means recognizing that women suffer more. when human development is inadequate. As DAWN elaborates (p 21):

A gender perspective means recognizing that women stand at the crossroads between production and reproduction, between economic activity and the care of human beings, and therefore between economic growth and human development. They are the workers in both spheres – those most responsible, and therefore with most at stake, those who suffer the most when the two work at cross purposes, and those most sensitive to the need for better integration between the two.

The implications of this understanding are that a gender perspective has to be integrated at the highest policy levels and that women need to be strengthened in order to be able to hold economic and political policies and systems accountable. In addition economic alternatives that women have themselves been creating need to be supported and strengthened. One way of assessing the prospects for the achievement of a gender sensitive, people-centred development in a particular context is to have one typical woman as a yardstick against which actions are measured. This I do throughout the text by introducing Mrs Khosa as an average South African woman.

Fundamental transformation is urgent as South Africa, among comparable middle-income developing countries, has one of the worst records in terms of social indicators (health, education, safe water, fertility) and amongst the worst records in terms of income inequality. Poverty in South Africa has a strong "race" and gender dimension. Nearly 95% of the poor are black, 5% are coloured, less than 1% are indian or white[2]. The kinds of realities that have to be transformed are captured in the following quote by Mrs Khosa (a pseudonym):

My husband lost his job about five months ago... then two months ago I lost my job. We were desperate. There was no money coming in now.... Now they've cut off the electricity and we're two months in arrears with rent. They're going to evict us, I'm sure, we just can't pay though. My husband decided to go to Jo'burg... I don't know where he is... Sometimes (the children) lie awake at night crying. I know they are crying because they are hungry. I feel like feeding them Rattex. When your children cry hunger-crying, your heart wants to break. It would be better if they were dead. When I think things like that I feel worse... I'm sick... I can't take my children to the doctor when they're sick because there's no money... What can one do? You must start looking. You can also pray to God that he will keep you from killing your children[3].

As Mrs Khosa's experience shows, poverty in South Africa is linked with high unemployment, hunger and malnutrition, inability to pay for – or lack of access to – health care and basic services, disintegration of families, vulnerability, risk of homelessness, and sometimes despair. The burden is also greater on women than men, and children are the victims.

To turn around the poverty-stricken reality of 70% of the population will take both a long time, the political will, and a great deal of resources. It is the ultimate challenge of the Reconstruction and Development Programme (RDP) of the government and adult education and training.

The RDP is an ambitious framework which aims "to meet basic needs, develop human resources, build the economy and democratise the state and civil society". Underpinning the RDP is a strong concern with redress, equity and economic development. As adult education and training is integral to social, economic, political and cultural development, it is centrally involved in the RDP and therefore implicated in its success or failure.

For adult educators and trainers the South African case is not of parochial interest only. It provides the space to examine the political and social contexts within which learning occurs and to ask searching questions about the social purposes and the provision of adult education and training globally. We can do this while acknowledging that global similarities are rooted and shaped in national and historical uniqueness.

In this paper I begin by presenting an overview of adult education and training in South Africa and then proceed to give preliminary suggestions for adult educators who wish to enhance the possibilities for a more radical social and economic programme to succeed which will improve the life chances of Mrs Khosa and others like her.

AN OVERVIEW OF ADULT EDUCATION AND TRAINING IN SOUTH AFRICA

Adult education and training in South Africa have been shaped very directly by colonialism, capitalism and apartheid. The major actors within the history are organisations of civil society, including trade unions, nongovernmental organisations (NGOs) and community-based organisations (CBOs), the state and business. The history is one of simultaneous activities, often in direct conflict with one another, being driven by different social, political and economic interests[4]. There has been an active policy on the side of all previous governments to ensure that black people were not educated to participate fully in the society. A single quote by Cecil John Rhodes (1887) will illustrate the historic roots of the attitude of white domination that has been continued as official policy until 1994:

I will lay down my own policy on this Native question. Either you have to receive them on an equal footing as citizens, or to call them a subject race. I have made up my mind that there shall be class legislation, that there must be pass laws and peace preservation acts and that we have to treat Natives where they are in a state of barbarism in a different way from ourselves. We are lords over them. These are the policies of South Africa.... We have given them no share in the government and I think quite rightly too[5].

Given this history, the new democratic dispensation finds very poorly developed state policies and infrastructure for adult education and training.

Also within the economy, adult education and training have never been supported strongly. Incentives to encourage spending on training the workforce have been few. For many decades, as the industrialisation of the economy occurred, the need for skilled people has been met by the importation of skilled white immigrants from Europe, requiring little investment in education and training by companies. During the 1980s, because of economic need and pressure from the trade unions, adult education and training have gained in prominence in the workplace. During the 1990s, several trade unions have had education and training demands as part of their negotiations with employers. The Congress of South African Trade Unions (COSATU) has given important leadership in the shaping of policy debates during the early 1990s.

It is within civil society that there is some of the richest history of adult education[6]. Much of the adult education activity has been part of a struggle against class and "race" oppression. It has been mainly of an informal and nonformal kind within different social movements.

Throughout the history, the worlds of adult education and training have barely communicated with one another. Trainers have been located mainly within the formal economy and adult educators have been working within organisations of civil society. Adult educators have generally been concerned with various aspects of social, political and community development while trainers have focused on "human resource development" within the formal economy.

In societies in a transition from authoritarian to democratic rule there are high expectations about how society ought to be organised. There is democratic political engagement and optimism about change. Mass mobilisation is a crucial element in transition societies and education is a primary means to attain this. The legitimacy of the new democratic state depends on the citizens' acceptance of the hegemony of its ideology. Its legitimacy also relies on its ability to raise the material consumption of the population. Adult education and training are important to these processes. Particularly in societies moving towards 'socialist policies' adult education, as part of a process of political mobilisation, has been critical to reaching out to the marginalised adult population in order to incorporate them into the newly defined nation[7].

In order to assist with the radical reform of the society, adult education and training have to work to consolidate and deepen democracy and to strengthen the economy, all within a framework of 'globalisation from below'. The ultimate measure of success should be in the impact it makes on the lives of people like Mrs Khosa and her family.

WHAT ARE THE PRIORITIES FOR ADULT EDUCATION IN SOUTH AFRICA?

1. The Reconstruction and Development Programme (RDP)

While there has been widespread support for the RDP there is a growing disquiet, especially from the left that there is now too much emphasis on economic growth as opposed to development and redistribution. A new macro economic strategy has been accepted which foregrounds economic growth above meeting basic needs. Descriptions of problems and achievements of the RDP are beginning to emerge.

There are major contradictions in the RDP which is a national effort to both reconstruct and reconcile a nation of very diverse interests. While it is too early to assess the RDP it is clear that at an ideological level it remains an extremely important instrument to legitimise the fight against poverty, inequality and injustice. A very important priority for adult education and training is to raise the consciousness of the broad population concerning the RDP and the critical contestations over paradigms of development that are imbedded within it. The RDP is committed to people-centred development-important questions to probe are: development for which people and to what end?

Although the new Bill of Rights states that, 'The state may not unfairly discriminate directly or indirectly against anyone on one or more grounds including race, gender, sex, pregnancy, marital status, ethnic or social origin, colour, sexual orientation, age, disability, religion, conscience, belief, culture, language, and birth', it is a fact that South Africa is a patriarchal, homophobic, racist society. Therefore, the ideals within the Bill of Rights will only be achieved through the struggle of different interest groups to ensure that their rights become reality.

In South Africa there has been a very rich history of "struggle politics" over many decades. A vast array of civil society organisations played critical roles in the political transformation. During those years the connection between "the struggle" and "development" was not made. There is generally a very conservative notion of development which is often equated with the expectation of delivery of basic material goods and services. While there is this perception the possibilities for people-driven development are slim.

Adult educators can play a role in making the connection between the discourse of development and the discourse of struggle. It is essential that more and more people, particularly women, realise that to change their economic, social and political realities will still take concerted, collective actions by communities and groups. But whereas before civic actions were always directed against the apartheid state, now democratically elected government officials may at times also be allies. The dualistic thinking of 'them and us' that prevailed during 'the struggle', which related to 'state and non-state', needs to become more nuanced.

The historical role of adult education to help mobilise marginalised and disadvantaged communities to resist and to claim a better deal for themselves is still a priority.

2. Education and Training for Democratic Participation

A new democracy takes years to consolidate and is very vulnerable. The consolidation and deepening of democracy requires behaviour and institutional changes at every level of society, from the biggest to the smallest social units, within civil society including the family, the state, and the economy. From a gender perspective it needs to involve both the ongoing development of gender sensitive facilitative legal and policy frameworks within which democratic participation can occur, and the development of capacity for various constituencies and individuals to participate effectively, particularly for women.

A Micro Organisational Focus

A key question for adult education is how organisations within civil society are to build their capacities to engage effectively in multipartite structures. In a previous study of education for democratic participation, I found that both the means and the ends of the organisations were very important. The participatory democratic practices were central to ongoing human development which is so critical to their functioning. Also the organisations' connections to other similar organisations as part of a social movement were essential to ensure that democratic practices did not become ends in themselves but were focused on bringing about change in the broader society. From a feminist perspective this means being connected to the women's movements.

In the last five years the emphasis on participatory democracy within civil society organisations has weakened with, for example, the pressure for NGOs to 'professionalise', become more efficient, and deliver services on a bigger scale. They are having to compete with one another in the marketplace which makes competitive individualism more dominant than notions of collectivism. There has also been a lessening of accountability to a social movement. Many activists from the democratic movement have been absorbed into government. Although there have been the emergence of several more specialised, focused groupings and social movements to which many organisations within civil society are aligned. For example, a large coalition of women's organisations from across the political spectrum formed themselves into the National Women's Coalition which was concerned with impacting the national constitution making process and the development of a Women's Charter. The future of the WNC is not certain at this point.

It seems that within all organisations of the society participatory democracy is an important element which needs to be encouraged in order to build self-confidence, leadership capacity, and train democrats. It is clearly not a straight forward matter and would need to be shaped by its particular social and organisational contexts. But in South Africa which is in desperate need to build human capacity it needs to be accepted as a general principle.

Long term organisational development work would be required to educate and train participants in organisations in order to achieve effective participation at all levels. Part of these processes would include training related to challenging racism, sexism and other forms of chauvinism. Another aspect would involve rethinking organisational policies and practices which may reinforce particular classed, raced or gendered power.

A Macro Focus

In the transitional period, education for democratic participation has involved various state structures. On the one hand, the state has been developing the democratic constitution, laws and institutional structures in order to provide a democratic framework. Institutions like the Human Rights Commission and the Gender Commission have been established and are in different stages of development. Specific education processes have also been undertaken.

There have been some impressive adult educational programmes that have been run in the last two years through the state and civil society organisations. For example, voter education to educate and mobilise the vast majority of the adult population to vote in the first democratic elections in 1994 was a major undertaking. The next major educational task was to involve the population in the national constitution-making process. The Constitutional Assembly conducted workshops, public meetings, utilised media to involve millions of individuals and thousands of organisational structures in the development of submissions for consideration in the constitution. Four million copies of the draft constitution were distributed and the Constitutional Assembly engaged in multi-media campaigns to elicit participation of the public. Another Public Education Programme has been initiated by parliament which is concerned with building democracy. There are organisations within civil society which have similar aims but also have a watchdog function.

These state and civil society educational initiatives are extremely important. But if we remember the daily life experience of Mrs Khosa we need to ask how far any of the discussions or initiatives described thus far are going to impact on her reality? A major consideration is the distribution of financial resources in a way which benefits her.

An initiative which potentially is significant relates to the formation of a "women's budget". The idea behind this is to enquire whether each state programme or department at local, provincial or national level is impacting on women for the better. As Pregs Govender states[8]:

What we want to know is: who gets the jobs? what is the nature of the jobs that are being created? who gets the housing? what types of homes and communities are being developed? who gets the land? etc. Due to their different locations in the family and in the economy we want to know in what way tariffs, industrial relations, employment and industrial policy impact on women.

This initiative aims to demystify the economy for women, to set up indicators for judging the national budget, and for evaluating the performance of the different departments and programmes from the perspective of poor women. The initiative is aiming to influence the way the national budget is drawn up, how government functions, and to draw in civil society organisations in the research, education and lobbying processes. It identifies both the political and the economic spheres as crucial in order to make a difference to the life of a person like Mrs Khosa.

Another broad environmental concern that impacts on the possibilities for democratic participation particularly, but not only, of women, is that of the levels of violence at home, in the community, and at the workplace. A certain amount of education and training may assist women to deal with violence, but social and political conditions will be critical in the ability of people to move about freely without fear of physical abuse.

Closely related to education for democratic participation is education for development. In order to consolidate and deepen democracy the appalling levels of inequality and injustice have to be reduced.

3. Education for Development

Adult education has traditionally been concerned more with social, political, personal and cultural development than economic development. This has begun to be recognised as a major limitation as for many adults the primary concern is economic survival. We have seen that Mrs Khosa, like 50% of the poor in South Africa, is unemployed. In a recent survey amongst a cross section of South Africans the need for jobs was rated the top priority where the government could help most, and for the rural poor, piped water is almost as high a priority. Economic development includes all aspects of the economy including the national budget, the formal and informal sectors.

A key initiative in the movement towards a new adult education and training system came from the formal economic sector and more particularly from the trade union movement. The unions realised that even radical improvement of the existing industrial training system would still hold their members in a second class position. Their members needed to improve their own skills and knowledge to get better jobs. They needed to improve educational and development opportunities in their communities to obtain a better life for their families and neighbours. They also needed to contribute to a more productive and world competitive economy to pay for these policies. In the early 1990s the trade union movement joined employers and the state on the National Training Board and after three years of discussion, debate and negotiation they made policy proposals in 1994. These had "integration" as the cornerstone of national policy development, insisting on equivalence of adult basic education, vocational training and schooling.

One of the proposals was for a national qualifications grid, the National Qualifications Framework (NQF), which would secure integration, equivalency and access across a new national education and training system. A broad competency model was adopted to define and assess learning outcomes at all levels of the NQF.

Changing entrenched divisions between education, training and development systems is no easy matter. We are not only dealing with decades of apartheid but also with centuries of the division of the hand and brain which is deeply imbedded in Western philosophical traditions. These issues are obviously not South Africa's alone, and other countries with widely different political histories nevertheless face similar issues in education, training and development.

In South Africa the human capital theory seems to be dominant in the policy debates. There is concern amongst some adult educators in South Africa that the integration debate is being driven by interests in the formal economic sectors, by both organised labour and employers. But it is in the informal sector that most people work. If policies are developed with only the formal sector in mind, people like Mrs Khosa will in all likelihood not benefit. This concern is not to deny the critical importance of adult education and training for highly skilled, high level people.

The question of integration is an important one which has opened up spaces to engage different traditions and to potentially challenge the human capital notion. In the structures of the NQF, in the designing of outcomes-based curricula, in the teaching methodologies, in all aspects of the teaching and learning processes, there need to be struggles to ensure that the human capital and technicist views do not become predominant. Many of the concepts can be interpreted in conservative or progressive ways. At present the power of the concept of integration lies in the fact that opportunities are being created for practitioners 'to live in the gaps' between sectors and traditions of education and training. It is, for example, forcing community adult educators to take the needs of economic development seriously, and workplace trainers to remember the needs of a democratic civil society.

With structural adjustment programmes which are encouraging changing employment patterns, growing insecurity of employment, the reality of jobless growth, more and more people are having to make ends meet in the informal sector. This is true both in South Africa and elsewhere. This is happening at a time when state social welfare services around the world are being eroded. This means that any education and training policies and practices need to take the realities of people, particularly women, in the informal sector very seriously. The relationships between the formal and informal sectors are also important as people move from the one to the other and increasingly the formal sector is outsourcing work to informal sector businesses. So the divide between the two seems to be lessening. The divide between civil society and the economy is also diminishing.

An example of this is the increasing recognition of the importance of traditional economic institutions in poor communities, such as credit clubs, burial societies, and producer and consumer cooperatives. These are important for survival purposes, for solidarity and for their potential for deepening the practice of democracy. Many of them have not developed beyond survival mode and with support and sensitive intervention potentially they could provide more substantial economic support and a place for education and training in democratic participation, skills, social issues, for the grassroots membership. Many of these associations are run by women and could potentially be important sites for women's empowerment.

So far this section has concentrated on economic development, but I have tried to show that this includes a wide range of practices within the formal and informal sectors and indigenous voluntary associations. If we think of the lived reality of Mrs Khosa again it is very clear that it is not possible to keep economic activities separate from other social, political or cultural aspects, or to keep the economic, state or civil society sectors apart.

It is important to have a comprehensive approach to development. It must include economic concerns, but also those of health care, water and sanitation, family planning, environmental issues, and personal development. This latter area includes spiritual, cultural and religious matters. Religion plays a fundamental role in the lives of the majority of South Africans, including Mrs Khosa, in providing a meaning for life. This aspect of society is very important both for development and democracy.

People's centred development is underpinned by a radical humanism which incorporates the struggle for equality and economic development. Galtung[9] argues that in societies in which people's personal domains in which they can feel needed and loved are torn apart there is a need for rehumanising the vast impersonal institutions of modern society. In South Africa the need to strengthen and support the development of what Galtung calls a 'culture of compassion' is very important. Mrs Khosa and her family, and others like her, desperately need to experience that. Closely linked to this is the growth of a culture of tolerance. Initiatives like the Truth and Reconciliation Commission, which is currently sitting in South Africa, are very important in this regard.

IN CONCLUSION

The central question for this paper has been what adult education and training should focus on in order to enhance the possibilities for a more people-centred social and economic programme to succeed in South Africa at a time when global economies dictate neo-liberal policies as the only acceptable solutions. Put another way, what would need to change for Mrs Khosa and her family's life circumstances to change?

The processes of globalisation are encouraging social fragmentation. The opposite of globalisation is localisation. This paper has argued that adult education and training is integral to economic, social, political, and cultural development which needs to rebuild social cohesion at the local levels, taking very seriously as its starting points the daily lived realities of people like Mrs Khosa.

Simultaneously, because the local is shaped so powerfully by the global, solidarity and a culture of compassion need to deepen at both local and global levels. The need for building solidarity in a climate of competition is a crucial part of alternative strategies to increase levels of the rights and living standards of the majority. Globalisation from below, which means the building of solidarity and collective action amongst civil society organisations and movements, needs to take place across a wide spectrum of social causes. Adult education and training are integral to these social processes.

NOTES

1. DAWN Markes on the way: The DAWN debate on alternative development. DAWN's platform for the Fourth World Conference on Women in Beijing September 1995
2. Ministry in the Office of the President: RPD "Key indicators of poverty in South Africa". Saldru, October 1995
3. op cit "Key indicators of poverty"
4. See Cathy Gush and Shirley Walters: *"Adult Education and Training in South Africa. A selected chronology from 1910 to 1995."* CACE, UWC, October 1995, for a brief overview of the history
5. Quoted in Dr Alex Boraine: *"The legacy of the past: South Africa"*. Paper presented to a conference on Comparative Analysis of Transition in Chile and South Africa. Cape Town, November 1995.
6. Rich examples of these are described in Clive Millar, Sarah Raynham and Angela Schaffer 1991: *Breaking The Formal Frame: Readings in South African Education in The Eighties.* Oxford University Press, Cape Town; also Shirley Walters 1989: *Education for Democratic Participation,* CACE Publications, UWC, Bellville
7. Martin Carnoy and Joel Samoff 1990: *Education and Social Transition in The Third World*, Princeton University Press, USA
8. A speech by Pregs Govender, a member of Parliament, reported in "Women's Health News" May 1996, No. 18, Johannesburg
9. Johan Galtung *"On the social costs of modernisation. Social disintegration, atomie/anomie and social development"* in *Development and Change* Vol. 27, No. 2, April 1996. Blackwell Publishers, England

Adult Learning, Human Rights and Democracy in Africa

Dani W. Nabudere

Learning About What?

The Whole concept of adult learning raises immediate questions: Learning? Learning about what? Why learn when I have no need for it? These questions on the surface look superficial but when they are examined within particular cultural-historical contexts have deep meaning. They have even more significance when they are raised in relation to learning as "adult literacy": Learn to write, read and numeracy for what?

To be sure, the mainstream attitude to adult education and adult learning in Africa has been hostile, ambivalent, and at best paternalistic. Even the concept itself became contentious and ambiguous to policy makers themselves. Today we define adult education as:

"the entire body of organized educational process, whatever the content, level and method, whether formal or otherwise, whether they prolong or replace initial education in schools, colleges and universities as well as in apprenticeship, whereby persons regarded as adult by society to which they belong develop their abilities, enrich their knowledge, improve their technical and professional qualifications or turn them in new direction and bring about changes in their attitudes and behaviouur in the twofold perspective of full personal development and participation in balanced and independent social, economic and cultural development." (Terminology of Adult Education, Ibedata, UNESCO/IBE 1979).

This definition is too broad and shows the complexity of the problem. First, it assumed the existence of an "organised educational process" which takes into account the educational needs of the "adult". Even then the above Ibedata definition also has difficulties with the term and defines "adult" as "a person who has reached physical and intellectual maturity" which itself also introduces new complexities. Secondly, the definition also assumes that the society where the "adult" so defined is situated has created processes for the "intellectual and personal" development of the person, whatever method and content of such an education.

The experience in Africa would suggest that such an understanding is highly problematic and cannot be sustained. The question is why? Although we have argued that the issue is a complex one, the simple answer to this question is that the problem of learning as such is clouded with a lot of mythology and manipulation by the strong economic interests which exist within African societies. This has its roots in the colonial system, education was divided into compartments of informal education; formal education and non-formal education. These were separate and specialised institutions of learning. This compartmentalization also fitted in well with the economic needs of modern society.

In the colonial system, even the different channels of education were opposed to one another. The children of the peasantry (who constituted the vast majority of the population) who went to formal schools had first to be cleansed of the "bad habits" and "pagan beliefs" of their parents before they could follow a proper formal education. It is not that the religious education which they received was in itself "bad". The issue was that the pupil was being socialised to despise his roots and transform him/herself culturally into some new entity. This had even serious complications for the attitude which the new political set up had for the peasant parent himself. He was considered to be a degraded "ignorant" specie who could only be "redeemed" if he converted him/herself into a christian or moslem. As such he or she did not have anything to offer to the child who had to be brought up in new civilised-christian ways. This was the first infringement of basic human rights and became the basis for the struggle of the colonial peoples against colonialism.

The second problem with the three tier categorisation of education is that once one had undergone the formal education, say, to the University level, that was the end of learning and the beginning of working. There was a chasm between the two worlds although in reality one continued to learn as he/she worked. But there was an even more fundamental problem with this approach. The majority of the peasants who were expected to produce what was required in the "Mother" country, remained without any formal education which could have enabled them to become "intellectually mature". In fact it is doubtful if this could have happened given the very motivations of colonialism in its quest for super-profits. Formal education was provided for a minority who filled certain positions in the colonial civil service and those who went to the very top of the educaitonal system were a much smaller minority of that minority. The result was that you had a pyramidical "organised educational process" which was highly segregated and segmented against the vast majority of the population. If education was to be regarded as a basic human right under the second generation of rights and freedoms, then it is clear that its denial to the majority of the population was a violation of their rights. But this is gainsaying the obvious!

The pyramidical structure of organised education meant that the peasant adult was left out of the "system" of learning and left to his/her own devices. In fact education in the formal sense was considered "harmful" since it might make him/her more enlightened to make political demands on the powers that be in return for his/her labour which was being "offered" almost free of charge. Indeed from this standpoint education was conceived as being "subversive" of the interests of the colonial political economy. The segregation and denial was intended to make him/her continue his "ignorant" role of clearing and tilling the fields with the crude sickle and hoe to produce the colonial products required of him/her.

This did not however mean that the "ignorant" peasant was not given an "education" of his iwn suited to his/her role. He/she in fact was surrounded by a battery of colonial officialdom, including chiefs and agricultural assistants, who taught him how to grow and look after the crops which was required for export. They did not need any education about their subsistence crops since the knowledge about these was readily available to them and passed on through another system of education – the traditional system of integrated functional livelihood. So for all practical purposes, the "ignorant" peasant was only good as a producer of cash crops for which he was given an adequate "informal" education on the field through extension services. Besides this he/she had no other channels except the church, where if he/she was lucky in accepting Christianity he/she might be taught to read the Catechism and in that way become "literate" capable of reading the bible.

The State and the Culture of Civil Rights

This colonial approach was not accidental nor was it contrived. It had its roots in the rationale and roots in the ideologies of "progress", "modernization", "enlightenment" and "redemption", of which the colonial enterprise was just part. Education throughout the "civilised world" was segmented in the same way and further compounded by various levels of "specialisations". This development merely reinforced the colonial enterprise which pushed the peasant down the ladder where education for enlightenment and self-improvement as well as civil rights was denied and made inaccessible. As we have stated above, this was denial of such a right and it arose with the introduction of colonial-modernity in Africa.

Indeed this could not have been otherwise. The colonial state itself was an imposition on the people of Africa. It was an extension of an already developed imperial state with different kinds of administrative and coercive departments responsible for the administration and exploitation of the colonies. The imperial state was therefore an "over-developed liberal state" when it was exported to Africa and other parts of the colonised world. Once exported to the colonies, the colonial state itself became an "over-developed colonial state" in relation to its population.The population was not civil society because the state did not emerge in response to their struggles and aspirations as was the case with the revolutions of Europe which brought about the creation of modern nation-states.

The colonial state did not develop along with the fulfilment of peoples' aspirations like it did in Europe. On the contrary it came to the colony *already developed to deny them any aspirations other than those desired by the colonial state*. It was therefore an oppressor state which could not have even countenanced the emergence of any civil society. Civil society was the enemy, an antithesis of the colonial state. It was precisely the task of the overdeveloped colonial state to block the emergence of such a civil society in the colony.

It was not therefore surprising that adult learning which advanced the enjoyment of human rights did not arise since *democracy was denied as a matter of course*. The colonised *peasant was not a subject and citizen within the state with any rights* but an imperial object of imperial subjugation. If he/she was referred to as a "subject", it was in the sense of him/her being a *subjected* person. Citizenship belonged to those in the "Mother" country and not to the "subject peoples" in the colonies.

The post-colonial state inherited all the attribues of the "over-developed" institutions and structures of the colonial state. The post-colonial state was already "sensitized" in the art of repression and exploitation of the peasantry since it was tied to the mechanisms of colonial plunder which did not change with the achievement of political independence. Although the creation of the new states was the result of the struggles of three main components of the colonial society: the peasantry, the workers and the "middle classes". It was the latter who became the wielders of local political power on behalf of "the people". In what Basil Davidson has called *The Blackman's Burden* the African post-colonial nation-state became a "curse" to its people almost immediately on its emergence with the achievement of political ("flag") independence.

The anti-colonial struggle sought to do away with the exploitation of the peasantry and the workers. Each of these social classes demanded "fair prices", "higher wages" and "equal rights" for all. The "middle classes" demanded better colonial jobs as well as better promotional prospects in the colonial service. The denial of these demands created a "national feeling" of oppression. When the demands could not be met, a "national" coalition of these forces calling itself a "national democratic/liberation movement" emerged. This alliance arose on the basis of the above "social agenda" comprising the demands of each of the social classes. According to Basil Davidson the agenda meant that: "There should be education for all, health services for all, opportunities for all; and these blessings would bind up the wounds of the colonial past and present, and bring a new life that must in every positive sense become modern life." (*The Blackman's Burden: The Curse of the African Nation-state.* 1992).

But the economic and social conditions of the peasantry and the workers, as well of those of the lower ranks of the "middle-class" could not be met in any sustained way. The economic conditions in the world market, especially relations with the former colonial markets which continued to dominate the economies of the post-colonial "independent states" were still oppressive and exploitative of these producing social forces in the former colonies. Prices of primary commodities continued to fall relative to prices of imported manufactured goods which continued to rise. It was reported that Africa had lost $ 19 billion in a single year in export prices while the cost of manufactured goods which had been imported to African countries had risen by 14 per cent. The "terms of trade" worsened and wide fluctuations in prices of African primary commodities made it impossible even to "plan national development". In these circumstances it is not surprising that African leaders found it increasingly difficult to address the social agenda. Basil Davidson has observed:

"While the outside world stood by and continued stolidly to take its cut of Africa's productive wealth, giving back less and less in grants, aid, or better prices, the scope for political redress (within Africa) correspondingly narrowed. As the new nation-states lost their legitimacy in the eyes of widening ranks of citizens, and hunger spread with less and less means of relieving it, there came what everyone could see.... to be a steady decline in the moral and political values of those who led or claimed to lead the nation-states." (Ibid.)

But the second item on the agenda of national liberation that of the nation-building had to be continued against all these odds because this was a continuity of the colonial mission. As the social agenda was more or less abandoned and the peasants were argued to "eat grass", the ruling middle-class elites who had fought for better colonial jobs and better promotional prospects in the colonial service and who now came to lead "or claimed to lead the nation-state", swore to continue with this agenda even if it meant that this had to be done without civil rights. The agenda had attained a self-propelling rationale built within the colonial system which the new leaders had inherited along with the colonial state structures.

It should not be assumed that this task too had not been a task of the colonialists. Sir Hilton Poynton, a former administrative head of the British Colonial Office, while speaking at a Cambridge symposium, reminded those assembled that the objectives of British colonial policy could be summed up in one word: "Nation-building". To him what Britain had engaged in all along in the colonial era was to "build" separate nation-states as the successors and inheritors of colonial states. This was seen as necessary in order to ensure "continuity" of the colonial project. (Basil Davidson: Blackman's Burden). For the colonial administrators, the colonial constitutional reform which became necessary in the wake of African nationalism, according to Dennis Austen, was essential to "enable colonial rule to be (made) more effective and not to hasten its demise."

Thus it can be seen that the agenda of "nation-building" did not any longer require the anti-colonial alliance with the peasantry and the workers in the new post-colonial state. The economic and social bases of their organisations had been weakened and destroyed by the economic decline and exploitation built within the imperialist world economy and the dictatorial political structures in the post-colonial states.

These dictatorial structures were now even more perfected under the dominance of the ideology of "nation-building" which attained a priority over the "social agenda". The peasants became increasingly desperate while the workers were being "retrenched" in large numbers to join the ranks of the impoverished peasantry in spiralling poverty. Their "cost" and "price" of social reproduction had fallen in the world market and at home they could easily be "bought" politically to cast their votes whenever these were required to legitimise the rule of the new rulers "on behalf of the people".

What this meant in real fact in terms of human rights and democracy was that none could be achieved or even advanced except formally. "National security and stability" became the new overwhelming policy positions of the state as the pursuit of the nation-building agenda became even more pressing. Whoever stood in the way of the government in its search for "national unity" and "stability" was regarded as an enemy of the state or "the people". The colonial reality of the "over-developed state" reappeared. It did not have its legitimacy from the people and instead it resumed the repressive role it had all along played. It did not exist for civil society: it stood against it.

The concept "the people" was now being used by the over-developed post-colonial state against the real people whom it claimed to represent and whom it had alienated and against whom it now stood. Colonial Emergency and Detention Laws were retained or were re-enacted by the new "independent" legislatures modelled on the Westminster or Paris Parliaments or Chamber of Deputies to check on any civil protests by the population in defence of their economic and social rights.

The possible emergence of civil society was being crushed in the bud. Political party freedoms were curtailed and their leaders and supporters imprisoned or banished into involuntary exile. One-party states and dictatorships soon replaced the Westminster and Paris modelled multi-party democratic systems. All this was considered necessary for the "national unity" which was essential for the nation-building project. Any educational activity aimed at strengthening peoples' basic human rights which were declared "inalienable" under the new "republican" constitutions was seen as "subversive" to the state and "the people". The chicken of colonial dictatorship had come home to roost except that this was now in the name of "the people".

Absence of Civil Society and Adult Learning for Citizenship

What has been said above shows that it is impossible in the case of the African post-colonial states to conceive of citizenship (in the sense of a liberal state) because citizenship cannot exist without the existence of a modern civil society whose organisations reflect the level of civil rights which they have achieved through their struggles. If the state is "over-developed", as we have argued above, then civil society is weakened to the same extent. The real question is whether one can conceive of a system of civic education which can advance the people's basic human rights, democracy and citizenship in such a state? This question also raises the problem of the legitimacy of such states since they claim to represent "the people".

In our view, the activities of civil society which reflect the aspirations of the citizens in the advancement of their interests implies a level of constant learning through political participation and participatory decision-making processes. This constitutes one of the pillars of democracy. A truly participatory democracy is one which recognises and protects the human rights of the people to engage in democratic and civic organisations to advance their interests. Political participation in this sense is also an empowering process in that it creates enlightenment and a sense of self-achievement for the participants. The creation of popular institutions of adult learning reflects the level of struggle of these different interests to improve their conditions. According to a document entitled "Civil Society and the Welfare State: Prospects and Challenges" submitted by the Israel state to the UN Social Summit in Copenhagen in March, 1995:

"The concept 'civil society' refers to uncoerced human associations that exist in the space between the family and the state, and which include rational networks of various kinds. The civil society, so it is argued, enables individuals and groups of individuals to assert their respective collective choises in matters of faith, forms of life, ideology, culture, social services, and economic affairs."

In African post-colonial societies where the state has "over-developed" before the emergence of a civil society, the state tries to create institutions "on behalf" of the people. These include institutions for "adult education". Adult education was introduced in Africa in these conditions as a "voluntary" activity organised by the state to "combat illiteracy".

The advancement of adult learning must have a purpose. If the structures and social and economic relations of modernity do not respond favourably to the needs of the vast majority of rural Africans, it is clear that adult education which is connected with the drive by the state to "eradicate or wipe out illiteracy by the year 2000" can never bear fruit. In the 1980s, it was realised by those in state authorities in the world that literacy on its own which aims at imparting basic reading, writing and numeracy skills cannot have real impact on society. It was then found that "follow-up" work and the procurement of "better reading materials" or "post-literacy" was necessary.

It was also realised that talking about literacy meant talking about "a whole range of educative services such as health and family planning, agricultural extension, post-primary skill training (e. g. in crafts skills for self-employment), community development and women's groups educational goals." This was also soon seen to be related to specific developmental needs of the community such as the need for hygiene, better husbandry or the generation of self-employment. Non-formal Education in this context now came to have three components: (I) literacy for adults and out of school youths; (II) Universal Primary Education-UPE; and (III) adult continuing education. All these were now regarded as necessary part of the package in "national development".

But this realisation is precisely what African post-colonial states had failed to achieve in their social agenda as we saw above. The failure of "national development" meant that mass literacy, UPE and adult continuing education could not be pursued effectively. It meant that the whole social agenda had aborted and the very basis of the African nation-state was openly challenged. Moreover, it is also questionable whether a non-formal system which included universal primary education was a realistic proposition, even if it could be financed. Such a system of schooling was culturally disarming and economically dis-empowering in that it would have created expectations which could not have been met. It is also questionable whether such schooling would have produced any learning at all for the adult masses.

To begin with, the mass literacy campaigns which were launched in a number of African states were misconceived because they were based on colonial carry-overs which held that the illiterates were "ignorant" and "backward". This is because a correlation was drawn between illiteracy and lack of economic development as such. Working on the western model of modernization which lacked depth, it was argued that the west had developed because the vast majority of the population were literate. From this it was easy to draw the conclusion that once illiteracy was "wiped out", development would follow, almost automatically.

In fact there was no historical basis for such a conclusion. While it was true that many illiterates in Europe for instance gained some level of literacy in the process of becoming christians, widespread literacy of the population came after the industrial revolution and then reinforced the industrial development of those countries. Education came to be achieved as part of the struggle for "social reform" which was pursued by civil society itself. Furthermore, there was no evidence to prove that the eradication of illiteracy, even if it was possible, could of itself remove poverty and bring about overall economic transformation. In fact the very process of trying to enforce "adult literacy" through massive campaigns led to the mystification of the realities and processes of modernization and created more ignorance on the part of the population who got "development fatigued" just as the donors too did get "aid fatigued". The two were interlinked. This is why a Nigerian adult educator has remarked:

"The issue of wiping out illiteracy in Nigeria has constituted as much a problem – possibly a disease – as the problem of illiteracy itself. Indeed, the problem has gradually become perennial and is almost acquiring a resistance to all prescribed solutions. After three earlier efforts to eliminate illiteracy, the persentage of illiterate people in the country now seems to have increased." (Michael Omelewa: "On the intractable question of literacy campaigns in Nigeria". In: Adult Education and Development. September, 1988).

He adds that illiteracy seems to increase because the Nigerian political elites have "benefited" from the existence of illiterate people in Nigeria. This is because the illiterates have remained "uninformed (of government policies and programmes) and are thus uncritical of government decisions", concerning their well-being: "Adult education was thus ignored by post-independence political leadership". From this it should follow that African political elites have an interest in having an "ignorant" population who are uninformed in order for the multinational companies to continue the exploitation of their populations from which the elites benefit. The suppression of people's human and democratic rights and denial of citizenship are built within the political economy of the post-colonial African nation-state.

The political process is riddled with manipulations of the population. Voting processes are mere formalities to enable the political elites continue in power. Change only comes through the barrel of the gun in ever continuing scrabbles amongst the different factions for power. Constitutions are made to deny basic human rights of the people and to mystify political processes. Uganda is a good example of this statement. Recently Uganda adopted a new constitution (the author of this paper was a member of the Constituent Assembly which debated and promulgated that constitution). Although a whole chapter was inserted in the constitution to protect people's basic human rights and freedoms, a number of articles were also inserted which nullified these freedoms.

It was argued by those wielding political power in the Constituent Assembly that inalienable human rights were "not absolute"; that they could not be regulated in the interests of "society as a whole". It was further argued that multiparty democracy and the right to organise freely through political parties was a privilege which could be controlled. A clause was inserted in the constitution which created a "new political system" called a "no party system" or "movement political system" which overrides the existence of political parties because this "new political system" is assumed to be "over-embracing, broad-based and non-partisan".

All Ugandans are expected to belong to the new system by constitutional and legislative fiat and not out of their choice. As long as this system exists political parties "remain in abeyance" and are prohibited from organising party branches, meeting or holding annual delegates conferences to elect party leaders. During presidential and parliamentary elections, political parties are not permitted to put forward any manifesto or platform for election nor are they allowed to put forward any candidates to contest elections freely. On the contrary, those who offer themselves to stand for public office do so "on their individual merit" and not on the basis of any alternative politics. Only a presidential candidate may put forward a policy framework.

Under these circumstances, elections are a mere "beauty/money contest" where aspiring candidates parade and show their faces at pre-arranged "candidates meetings" since none of them is allowed to hold a private meeting. Candidates are only allowed to hold "consultation meetings" with small groups of voters and not "rallies". After these "consultative meetings", the candidates go round dishing out money to the poor voters to procure votes from them. This also facilitates the political corruption, since the impoverished population are distrustful of these political elites, they draw the conclusion that they are merely choosing who amongst them is "going to eat". The poor people in many cases insist that candidates give immediate support to their "projects" and "today's food" before they are elected. The elites in any case encourage this kind of behaviour on the part of some of the voters by offering bribes for votes as pointed out. This is done to a people who are dis-empowered and who are mostly starving due to lack of development. Votes are counted in terms of money and not programmes for social advancement. Whoever is able to dish out as much money as possible is "elected"! Those holding political power have all the resources to achieve their political objectives.

What is said above was noted and complaints were lodged with the electoral commission during the 1966 presidential and parliamentary elections with no response. The practise was so widespread that even the electoral commission could not enforce the law which outlawed political corruption. Those holding important public offices were the ones using public funds and materials for bribing the populaton for votes. Voting cards were bought and taken away from voters. Other voters were bought to "vote correctly" for the preferred official "no party" candidates! Recently a presidential adviser publicly acknowledged this phenomenon which has become normal at a seminar when he stated:

"in our zeal to privatise everything we have monetized elections... Something must be done and done urgently if the movement political system is not to be discredited like its predecessors since independence."

He added that in some constituencies which he had observed, large amounts of money between 200 to 400 million shillings (200,000-400,000 US$) were disbursed ander the guise of food refreshments: "These things happened and the press exposed them but nobody in government is doing anything about it". It was clear that government could not do anything about it because those in authority were the ones perpetrating the corruption which increasingly undermined the democratic process. This if anything proves that human rights, democracy and citizenship cannot be realized in African conditions. Uganda despite these violations of basic human rights, has been praised by the international community of "donors" as having embarked on the road of democratisation and constitutionalism"! What a fallacy!

How the People Protect Their Rights and Enhance Their Learning in Their Own Environment

The above analysis should not give a one-sided view of the process of adult learning and its relation to human rights, citizenship and democracy. Since the African post-colonial state has failed to deliver its social agenda, the African people were left to their own devices to survive the effects of non-development and non-modernization. It is not that the people resisted all the benefits which arose from modernization: modernization on the people's own terms was simply excluded. Having been excluded they tried to live in two worlds all at the same time: the modern and the traditional worlds. In fact this duality is false viewed from the vantage point of the operations of the world economy. The modern world is linked to the non-modern world and vice-versa. The modern exploits the non-modern and is directly dependent on it. In the process the traditional gets hooked onto the modern "expert system" and survives side by side with it. It becomes in many ways a hybridization of itself and the modern world.

Nevertheless there is what can be referred to as the traditional mode of existence or at best, a "post-traditional" world, which most visibly manifests itself in the pastoralist communities of Africa. These "post-traditional" communities coexist with the modern mode of life and economy to which the latter is hooked. Even then, the traditional mode is clearly distinguishable from the modern mode and it is important to examine how the people have managed to maintain a semblance of civil life and civil existence under it. In its own trail, this "post-traditional" world has its own forms of informal and non-formal education which sustains their identity of the communities to the extent this is possible. It is through these means that they are able to learn about the need to respect other people's rights and to exercise some form of democratic life and "citizenship" at a clan or community level with others.

The failure of "modernization" in Africa is in fact the very reason why traditional values have persisted to a much greater extent than elsewhere in the world. It has meant the existence of traditional "civil society" based on different systems of adult learning which have remained in place or which have been created for survival needs of the community. The maintenance of traditional methods of medicine (herbs) and the knowledge associated with it is one example of the persistence of this form of traditional knowledge despite the dominance of western medicine and mode of treatment and healing. This knowledge is passed on to the initiates through a system of oral adult learning based on historical memory.

Adult learning must therefore not be confused with literacy or vice-versa as much as human knowledge must not be confused with book knowledge and vice-versa. Many African peoples have lived on this continent without having developed the art of writing or reading, but they have through orality and works of art and oral literature preserved their knowledge and cultures which have seen them through ages. In fact it can be said that until recently, the bulk of the people of the world did not know how to read and write and this privilege existed only for the upper classes – the literati of the feudal world. Much of the cultures of today's developed world came from these humble folk sources. Romanticism was a factor which went to strengthen modernisation in this sense.

It is therefore necessary to see how Africans have managed to sustain themselves and generate forms of knowledge which were suitable for their survival given the rather hostile atmosphere which was introduced by colonial modernity. The most important base for such a knowledge is the spiritual base. Through it the Africans associate themselves with perpetual existence through spiritual linkages with the ancestors. Africans do not engage in ancestor worship as is sometimes claimed by some westerns. They simply believe that through communication from their ancestors, they are able to understand reality and continue some form of knowledge by emulation and practice. Moreover their invisible links with ancestors enable them to surmount physical and psycological problems which have resulted in the alienation of the modern western person. This has resulted in the nihilistic and narcissistic responses to reality on their part. Spiritual ancestry is therefore a source of knowledge as well as a medium of transmission which is passed on in a form of adult learning. The spirit medium acts as both the link with the ancestors and a transmitter of such knowledge.

The knowledge preserved through orality in proverbs, stories, riddles, ballads, legends and folk-tales enables the poor African peasant to consult deep sources of knowledge which satisfies their desire for self-identity and social being. Through social being certain basic collective and individual human rights are preserved and respected, Citizenship in the ethnic or clan community is maintained on the basis of certain democratic principles of participation in decisions which affect their lives such as births, marriages, economic activity such as ownership or use of land, and death. Through proverbs in particular an assertion of values is buttressed and confirmed. A dialogue about relevance and meaning of the proverb or story in the changed conditions ensues and new parameters are established for new norms of cultural values and meanings.

For example, respect of other people's rights are expressed in a score of proverbs and tales. These act as a reminder, but also as an educational tool for the young who are initiated to this knowledge. In Lumasaba language of Eastern Uganda, for instance, when one evokes the proverb to the effect that *"Umwana nga akubire ingoma, bakulu nabo bakina"* meaning "when young people beat the drum, the old people must dance too", the idea is to buttress the respect of the views of the young people and by the same token to assert their rights in traditional setting. When it is invoked, everyone agrees with the appeal as a matter of course because it is believed that the proverb expressed a self-evident fact. If there is disagreement about the meaning to be applied to the proverb, dialogue issues until an acceptable meaning is arrived at.

A similar short story from Ghana when invoked also enables one to appreciate the importance of being modest. It expresses a disapproval of pretences to a monopoly of knowledge. It states that one day a foolish old man tried to collect all the knowledge in a village which he believed he alone knew and could preserve as his monopoly. He placed this knowledge in a calabash and tightly sealed it. He put the calabash on his back and climbed a tall tree with the objective of putting it away from the reach of anyone else. When he reached half-way up the tree, he realised he could not balance the calabash on a tree branch without it falling down. A young man who was standing below the tree laughed at the old man and told him to come down because he had an idea which could help him hang up the calabash. When the old man came down, the young man told him to take a long rope and tie it around the neck of the calabash. He advised him to tie a stone at the other end of the rope and then climb again and when he reached the highest point, he should take the rope and throw the stone around one of the branches. He should then pull the calabash up until it reached the desired height and then tie the rope around the trunk of the tree leaving the calabash to hang up. When the old man heard this advice, he realised he had not put all the knowledge in the pot and fearing that if he opened the calabash to include the latest knowledge of the young man, the other stored up knowledge might fly out, he decided there was no point in storing the knowledge in the calabash and putting it away since some other knowledge might not have been included in the calabash. Upon realising this he abandoned the whole idea of trying to have a monopoly on the knowledge which was a collective property.

The moral behind this story is that knowledge is not a monopoly of any one person. When told, just like the Lumasaba proverb, it evoked immediate approval from the community. It also acts as an educational method. The pedagogical implications are also clear: the knowledge which exists in the population in this form is as potent and vital as any, and perhaps more so than the written word. If used to re-awaken the population in certain deep humanistic values, it can help to enlighten them and motivate them into action oriented responses for self-improvement. The dialogue method which is implicit in the bringing to life this form of knowledge not only inspires those involved, it also empowers the individuals concerned for they can easily relate their activity to their basic human values enshrined in their deep consciousness. Moreover, it strengthens their cultural identity and enhances their dignity and self-respect which modern notions of the "ignorant illiterates" fail to capture. The methodology can be used side by side with other methodologies of adult learning which can have beneficial results which can lead to a literate population.

This explains why the post-colonial political elites are also hostile to people's spiritual and cultural values since they have been influenced by "modern" and christian spiritual and cultural values. They are blacks in white skins. They despise their cultural bases calling it "primitive" and "backward". Since they do not have faith in the creativeness of their own people because they regard them as "ignorant", they cannot motivate and inspire them into any of their "modernization" programmes of "economic development". These remain on paper as vast amounts of borrowed foreign money and locally generated resources through taxes are squandered on the conspicuous cunsumption life styles of the leaders who mimic and imitate western values. The people are left on their traditional values to survive the failed modernization.

Some Examples of People's Struggles for Human Rights

The case of the Ogoni people of Nigeria goes to show how a small community of 500,000 people was able to unite under their traditional values and institutions to fight for their human rights. The Movement for Survival of the Ogoni People – MOSPO – managed to bring together both the peasants and intellectuals such as the well known author and civil rights activist Ken Saro-Wiwa and others to stand up to the repressive and exploitative activities of the Nigerian military elites and the Shell multinational corporation. They demanded the right to a clean environment and a share in the profits from their oil resources. Through their civil rights organisation – MOSPO – they were able to raise the issues regarding their basic human rights in the post-colonial state of Nigeria and to challenge the very legitimacy of that state. The Ogoni people were also able to challenge the legitimacy of the economic activities of an international oil-monopoly – Shell – which was using the Nigerian state for its purposes against the interests of civil society. The murder of Ken Saro-Wiwa and his eight compatriots was intended to frighten the people into submission. Far from vanquishing the people in Ogoniland, the international response has been overwhelming in support of their cause and struggle.

The Ogoni struggle has also drawn attention to a number of very important issues which were assumed to have been resolved when the British colonialists put in place their "dual mandate". The creation of the Nigerian colonial-nation-state out of a disparate group of nationalities and ethnicities without their consent is being challenged. The Ogonis claim that they must regain control of their natural resources and their environment. This claim has raised the whole question of the right to self-determination of the Nigerian people as a whole. This claim is being linked to the vital issue of basic human rights, democracy and citizenship. The Ogoni's are asserting the right to determine their own future through their own institutions. They have used their traditions and cultures as a vital resource of strength to re-educate their intellectuals towards re-identifying themselves with the cause of the ordinary Ogoni peasants.

In a similar vein, immediately after the presidential and parliamentary elections in Uganda in May and June 1966, a small movement calling itself the Equatorial Nile Liberation Front – ENLF – was announced to have been formed in the North-Eastern Uganda region of Karamoja. This movement claimed to be representing five small ethnic communities of the region who have been marginalised by the Uganda post-colonial state. They claim the right to liberate themselves from the exploitative activities of "modernization" which were the key element in the electoral manifesto of President Yoweri Museveni. They claim that their ancestral lands have been taken over forcibly for purposes of mineral exploitation by a few individuals – both Ugandan and foreign. They claim these are their ancestral lands which they want to preserve against all costs.

The emergence of this small movement in Uganda is in sharp contrast to the other anti-government movements in the North and North-West of the country which have shown no clear political demands. The West Nile Bank Liberation Front also claims the right of self-determination and the right to separate from Uganda. A spirit of separatism can also be detected in the Buganda region in Central-South Uganda. This is a challenge to the legitimacy of the post-colonial state in Uganda.

The Ethiopian state has shown the way ahead in this respect by acknowledging the right of different nationalities in Ethiopia to vote through referendum to secede from the state if they so wish. The acknowledgement of this right by Ethiopia in fact recognises the crisis of legitimacy of the African nation-state and its future existence becomes fragile. The new Ethiopian constitution faces up to this challenge squarely by enabling the people to have an opportunity to reconstitute the state on a new basis. It recognises their right of self-determination below the line to the ethnic communities and nationalities instead of to the post-colonial nation state as such. This right was already tested even before the new constitution with the referendum in Eritrea in which the vast majority of Eritreans voted to become an independent state.

All these developments in Nigeria, Uganda and Ethiopia go to show that the people through their own cultures and traditions can raise important issues of common human concern. The support given to the Ogoni people internationally reflects this common human concern. In raising these issues, a global consciousness about these rights has been aroused and galvanised. The claim of the Ogoni peasants is seen to have a common human value.

Conclusion

In this paper, we tried to argue that forms of adult education in Africa have aborted because the very basis of the African post-colonial state, just like its colonial counterpart, has been to oppose the aspirations of the people. The failure of the "social agenda" meant that the African political elites were left with no option but to pursue the "nation-building agenda" which was a continuation of the colonial project. The pursuance of this agenda went a long way in resurrecting the "Law and Order" approach of the colonial state in relation to the general population and this led to an increasing denial of basic human rights.

Now unlike the colonial days, the new African nationalist leaders claimed to represent the people and all dictatorial policies which stood against the emergence of civil society and citizenship, were justified in their name. No longer could the people hope to exercise their aspiration of self-determination, because their basic human rights were violated in the name of the state or the people.

The very concept of education under these conditions has been questioned for even the formal education system is seen as creating unrealistic expectations on the part of the learners. In the end it is disempowering and disarming to the general population. The very concept of schooling is therefore put into question. On the other hand, it has been argued that the people who were left to their own devices have used the traditional systems and cultural values to maintain a semblance of civil society in the local settings by having recourse to certain traditional values expressed through proverbs, stories, etc. We have seen that this approach has enabled the people to challenge the very legitimacy of the states as well as the legitimacy of the activities of multinational corporations. This "post-traditional approach" is therefore empowering.

The condemnation of the formal school has also been re-echoed in western circles by the writings of people like Ivan Illich. He has argued for a new approach to education in the western countries –a system of education which permits learning to be undertaken outside the formal school system. This form of education also relies on the knowledge stored in the memories of the communities and although it cannot allow the possibility of a return to traditional methods, its argument comes nearer to the "post-traditional" approach we have noted above.

This means there are elements in both approaches that can rekindle the struggle of the people of the world for a more humanistic approach to education where "learning for learning's sake", according to Illich, is encouraged and where the contemptuous presumption that people are ignorant is dispensed with since the "ignorant" people become both the learners and the teachers of their peers.

Through humanistic re-mobilisation on a global scale through these and other means, the people of the world can once again be able to rekindle the bonds of common humanity in facing up to the destructive forces of economic globalization under way which the African nation-state represents. This is a process of global adult learning in defence human rights, democracy and global human citizenship which we should redefine and problematise for an effective global action.

Adult Learning and Democrazation in the Third World:

The Impact and Relevance of Grundtvig's Educational Ideas

Holger Bernt Hansen

The title of this paper, "Adult Learning and Democratization in the Third World" has been inspired by one of the themes at the forthcoming UNESCO Conference on Adult Education where the term adult learning appears. I am more familiar with the term adult education, whereas adult learning as a term and a concept is rather new to me.

When I find it useful to maintain the distinction between the two terms it is for the simple reason that within the area of development assistance adult education is often identified with the idea of equipping people with certain professional skills, in other words often identified with vocational training or in some cases with literacy courses. Adult learning is something different, it has to do with awareness-rising and consciousness-making. It represents the wider context of basic human values which are hardly measurable.

The distinction between adult learning and adult education does not represent an alternative, there is no insurmountable wall between them – hopefully they will work together in the sense that they can support and strengthen each other.

Provided that I am right in emphasizing such a distinction between adult learning and adult education it is significant that it is appearing at the present time. In my opinion it is related to the globalization process which we are faced with towards the end of the 20th century, and to be more specific it is related to one special aspect of the globalization process, the North-South relations. And to be even more specific, it has to do with the emphasis on human rights and democracy which constitute the most significant element in the North-South relations in the last decade of the 20th century.

Adult Learning and Democratization

The close relationship and even interdependency between the promotion of human rights and democracy on the one hand and the need for adult learning on the other will undoubtedly continue to be just as important in the first decade of the 21st century. But right now it represents a major challenge and a significant imperative for those of us who are working with development aid.

For some years I have been involved in both policy-making and implementation of the Danish development assistance, for the last year as chairman of the Danida Advisory Board. Since I joined the Board in 1987 the whole question of human rights and democracy has become of increasing importance. It has become a leading criterion when we select our programme countries, and it has in fact become one of the most important conditions or strings attached to the continued disbursement of aid to the recipient countries. Kenya versus Uganda in the Danish aid programme is a clear example of this mechanism.

I will pursue this line a little further. It has made those of us engaged in the development administration look at the environment in which a democracy will have to function. One first question has been: can any system of democracy function under conditions of great poverty and illiteracy? Does it make sense to call for or even demand elections under such conditions?

Our answer has been a yes, although expressed with some hesitance. We have been fully aware that we have to facilitate the process which we have done in three ways: first the aid has been geared towards some kind of economic growth accompanied by poverty alleviation; secondly we have strongly emphasized the need to support and allocate funds to the social sectors: health and not least education by which we are thinking in terms of formal education, primarily primary schools. But thirdly, and directly geared to the development of the democratic process, we have participated in voters' education, or we may call it civic education which means to make people aware of their rights and duties when voting and in general when acting within a democratic system.

In my opinion we are here engaged in adult education or better adult learning where we, as a donor agency, are working with NGOs, for instance churches and religious societies, with Human Rights organisations or just associations started for the sole purpose of conducting civic education.

This whole exercise is in the first place geared towards the process of democratization with a special focus on the election. But I would like to emphasize that the process of democratization is much wider and includes a number of areas. Democracy also represents a value system where each person has equal rights, and where those who rule follow a generally accepted code of behaviour. Transparency, the willingness to refute a monopoly of power, accountability for the funds spent, and so on. But it goes even deeper as it involves a respect for and adherence to the rules of the game in the sense that not just a top-down approach and mentality is prevailing, but also that there is room for a bottom-up approach, i. e. that the ordinary man in the village can influence the agenda, can dismiss the rulers and keep them responsible and accountable. In an African context we can say that the monopoly on power of the educated élite should be broken, and that the people in the villages be mobilized and be able to influence their own destiny. It is a change of relationship between those who rule and those who are ruled.

To me this is a major challenge which will take us far into the 21st century. This has meant that to a large extent we have engaged ourselves in adult learning geared towards this broadly conceived process of democratization which prevails in the North-South relations. But especially the support for democratization raises the issue whether in our approach, in our method of work and in our whole conceptualization of democracy we are acting from a commitment to western values, that we are indirectly or even directly exporting a western model of democracy.

This question is the more pertinent as we are approaching the turn of the century. The break-down of the communist system, the collapse of Eastern Europe and the end of the Cold War have given rise to an enormous western self-confidence. The western democratic system is seen as the victorious one which is the only safe road to progress for mankind. Now and again one is left with the impression that the support for democratization represents a crusade for western values towards the South. This again means that adult education or adult learning runs the risk of being too closely identified with a western bias to the exclusion of other interpretations which are embedded in local cultures and value systems.

Seen from the point of view of development work let me then draw a first conclusion. As we are moving towards the turn of the century we are in the North-South relations faced with a process of transition to democracy which again presents a great challenge to adult learning or adult education. There is a clear demand for adult learning, but at the same time there is a great risk of the donors imposing their own systems and values on the Third World countries.

Adult Learning as a Danish Speciality and Obligation?

The latter dilemma brings us to put special focus on Denmark as Denmark in particular is faced with the challenge to engage itself in adult learning at the present juncture of North-South relations, but at the same time Denmark is running the risk of imposing and exporting its own systems and experiences.

It is often claimed that for two reasons Denmark has a special obligation and a special gift to engage in adult education or adult learning in the developing world: first Denmark's unique historical experience from its own process of transition in the last half of the 19th century; secondly its unique ideological heritage based on the 19th century Danish theologian and educationist *N. F. S. Grundtvig* whose visionary ideas were put into practice in *the Folk High School movement* and the accompanying cooperative movement, both of which were instrumental in the transformation of Danish society.

These two arguments were in the forefront when Denmark as a non-colonial power first took an interest in the developing world around 1960. "The Folk High schools are our most important export product", it was emphasized. And the attitude is still the same. Only recently – at a meeting about the future Danish strategy for the agricultural sector – the complaint was made that the proposal for a new strategy had left out the special Danish method and approach, i. e. the cooperative movement. Within the same week one of the Danish newspapers carried a big headline, "Grundtvig as an export success".

Hence it is an important part of the Danish self-understanding that Denmark has a special message and a special obligation within adult education vis-à-vis the developing world. Representatives of this opinion are lobbying the administration, and in my opinion it is significant to what extent this whole attitude has become part of the general culture and the value system on the basis of which the decision-makers act.

And the special Danish obligation and the special Danish contribution have become even more topical in a period when democratization has moved to the top of the agenda. Hence it is often argued that Grundtvig's ideas and way of thinking are highly relevant at the present juncture; that the Folk High School idea can be an important instrument in the whole process of democratization; and that the cooperative movement presents a training ground in democracy for ordinary people.

It is from this starting point that I will now turn to a more critical examination of this presumedly Danish comparative advantage in advocating and engaging itself in adult education or adult learning.

The Heritage from Grundtvig

Let me start by saying that it makes perfect sense to include Grundtvig and revive his ideas in the present age of democratization. For Grundtvig the challenge was to equip and train people to function in a democratic system. It is important to remember that Grundtvig is not at all interested in technicalities as to how a political system works, voting procedures, not even the constitution as such. He wanted to enable the common man, the peasant, to take part, and on that account he strongly opposed the dominance of the élite.

For Grundtvig the common man was in the forefront, it was he who should be awakened, be made aware of his own resources, his own potentials. He should no longer be under tutelage, under the tyranny of the élite. He should be awakened and be ready to take responsibility for his own fate and for his own people's fate. He should be able to judge for himself and not be at the mercy of more learned people. When it comes to human relationship, knowledge is just not enough.

Connected with the awakening of man, the awareness-making process, was another principle which was just as important: there should be sufficient room for people to use their abilities and take responsibility for their own fate. It means that the principle of freedom should prevail in man's whole life. Freedom of speech, freedom of gathering and forming associations, freedom to print and publish. And the freedom should be combined with tolerance, with respect for other people's right to act.

In order to make people able to use the freedom and take responsibility for their own lives it was essential to educate people. Not for any special trade or profession, but simply "education for life", to awake people and make them conscious of their position in history and in relation to fellow human beings. And to fulfil this a purpose Grundtvig invented the Folk High School institution, the idea of adult education, to enable people to be conscious of their own abilities and potentials and take responsibility for their own fate and for the society they were living in, in short to live and function in a democracy. And the spoken word should be the most important means of instruction, not literary knowledge, not books.

It is important to emphasize that Grundtvig did not design and did not work for the introduction of democracy as such – that was not his real errand. His concern was to equip and to train people to live in a democracy and make use of its potentials. That was a major, though not the only function of the Folk High School institution.

It is just as important to keep in mind the distinction between democracy as a way of life and as a political system now that we live in a period when the western world – as I said earlier – is keen to impose democracy on the Third World countries. They seem to be thinking mainly in terms of the latter, democracy as a political system.

It is also important to remember that democracy in Denmark was not a result of Grundtvig's work alone, nor a result of the Folk High School movement. But the Folk High School had as its major task to make democracy work and to make it work better than would have been the case otherwise. In particular the Folk High School movement became of crucial importance in the consciousness-making of the rural population, of the peasantry. They made use of the freedom, and they became aware of their own potentials and rights, of their ability to take fate in their own hands. In spite of their limited literacy many peasants got the courage to challenge the authorities and to make changes, and in their villages they became pioneers in changing the way of production and in starting cooperatives, which helped to combine the peasant's traditional individualism with the advantages of working together in manufacturing and marketing their products.

This transformation, as it was, happened largely in the last half of the 19th century and early this century. I have to include a cautious note here. There are more than one factor involved in explaining the transformation of society and politics. But Grundtvig and the heritage from Grundtvig played a significant role. And looking back at this golden age of transformation, a number of people have said: this is unique, this should be exported, this very special process of political, social and economic change going hand in hand. And one place to start was to export the Folk High School idea and the idea of the co-operative movement.

Can Grundtvig and His Ideas be Exported?

This was tried at an early stage when in the 1950s Denmark for the first time had to define its relationship with the developing world or as it was called in those days the underdeveloped countries. At that time it was suggested by a number of people to link Grundtvig and the Third World. First of all, Grundtvig's ideas and their importance to the development in Denmark over the last century, not least adult education and more specifically the Folk High School movement, have presented answers and solutions which were considered very appropriate to the challenges facing Third World countries. It was not just the general idea of adult education and the importance of vocational training that generated the support. It was a belief in the Folk High School idea itself that it is a valuable instrument in a process of change and that it can become a mobilizing force in the face of the Third World's doubt and uncertainty as to the future pattern of development.

Correspondingly, there have been people in the Third World who at an early stage were responsive to the idea that Grundtvig has a relevant message for their particular situation. Let us go a little deeper into this by examining a few cases where attempts have been made to employ Grundtvig and the Folk High School idea in Third World countries. And one important question to keep in mind will be whether Grundtvig's conceptual framework and suggestions are applicable in a context which is quite different from the one Grundtvig was familiar with, and which is outside the Danish historical context.

One first case is naturally *Dr. Kachi Ozumba* and his Grundtvig Institute in Nigeria. Dr. Ozumba is one of the few Third World representatives who has actually studied Grundtvig and has become familiar with his ideas and not least the paradoxes inherent in the transfer of Grundtvig's ideas to the Third World in general to and Africa in particular. It is characteristic that Dr. Ozumba takes his starting point in Grundtvig's idea of alienation and uses it to interpret the situation in his own country. Just as Grundtvig fought "the Latin school" and the alienating Roman yoke, Ozumba has designated what he calls "the school for death" to be the enemy. The school for death was forced upon Nigeria and Africa as a whole as part of colonialism with all its alienating influences, and it was carried by the elite over and above the head of the man in the village. Naturally he turns to Grundtvig's idea of "education for life". The school for life must replace the school for death and must be aiming at awakening the popular dynamics and the people's own potentials by introducing what is called the awareness curriculum based on the living word and drawing on material from history, folklore, and traditional arts.

We can see how Dr. Ozumba applies Grundtvig's framework to explain and interpret the situation in the Third World in the aftermath of colonialism, and how he follows Grundtvig's means of alleviation by introducing the education-for-life concept. A little later we will discuss the problem to what extent the education-for-life concept can work in a post-colonial, Third-World situation. But it is important to emphasize that Dr. Ozumba does not ascribe any absoluteness to Grundtvig's thinking and ideas. On the contrary, he is fully aware that there has to be a translation process. "While Grundtvigian ideals can provide answers to most of our problems of development", Dr. Ozumba is fully aware that carbon copying will not work. It becomes a question of "exploring the potentials of Grundtvigian ideals" in the local community and keep ways and means flexible.

This is quite clearly a relative approach to Grundtvig's ideals and prescriptions, and by implication we may add that it takes account of the fact that the Nigerian situation and the African situation in general are set in a historical context different from the one Grundtvig faced in Danish society in his time. And implicitly we may further deduce that colonialism which most Third World countries have experienced meant a foreign hegemony and an alienating influence which penetrated and transformed the whole fabric of society to an extent which the Roman yoke could not manage in the Danish situation. This raises the question how applicable and of how much explanatory value Grundtvig's concepts will be in the longer term perspective; in other words, how adequate his categories will be. Dr. Ozumba has hinted himself at this question when in one place ends up by asking whether a Nigerian <u>folkelighed</u> is at all possible under the prevailing circumstances.

The Universality of Grundtvig's ideas

Over the years several attempts have been made to employ Grundtvig's universe and whole analytical framework in defining the situation of the Third World situation vis-à-vis the penetrating influence from Europe, not least by establishing a close parallel between the Danish situation in the 19th century and the Third World in the 20th century. Hence it would make sense to transplant the Danish model to the Third World in general and to Africa in particular. Like in Denmark earlier on, there is in Africa a high degree of alienation because of the foreign culture imposed from above by the elite.

Yet, it has to be questioned whether such an absolute approach to the transfer of Grundtvigian ideals and the direct linkage established between the 19th century Denmark and the 20th century post-colonial Africa is at all tenable. I will mention two issues for further consideration.

First, from the position of a historian, we must ask whether Grundtvig and the Grundtvigian ideals are at all transferable in the absolute sense we have met it here. Was Grundtvig not a product of a particular Danish situation and rooted in his special epoch? His basic concept was the nation as the undisputed and homogenous unit on the basis of which he could appeal to a given cultural tradition and expect the emergence of a coherent popular response. He had a stable and well defined basis from where he could operate. What happens when this is no longer the case? When the existence and function of the nation can no longer be taken for granted?

This leads to a second issue. It should be contemplated whether the colonial and post-colonial situation is not a sui generis situation which has no real parallels in earlier Danish history. A number of basic concepts are questioned. It is not just a problem of an imposed, foreign culture which undermines or denounces the national, popular culture. In the post-colonial situation we are faced with more or less imposed nations, artificially created, where the people's primary loyalty is hardly to the nation, but to smaller units like ethnic groups and religious communities. There are hardly any universally accepted institutions like the church which can integrate the newly created nation; there is no common historical experience which can justify the present state of affairs; and often there is no common language which can carry and unify the different cultural traditions. It is a situation of diversification which Grundtvig never had to face and could not take into account. Hence it has to be asked how and to what extent Grundtvigian ideals can work when transferred to conditions which are contrary to Grundtvig's own preconditions. In other words, the disruptive influence of colonialism goes far beyond the problem of an imposed, alienating culture, and questions the whole basis of operation.

The advocacy of the universality of Grundtvig's message and the argument for the relevance of the particular Danish experiences in a Third World situation are very useful, not least because it raises some pertinent questions about the use of Grundtvig and Grundtvigian ideals in meeting the demands for change in the Third World countries. It is of course easier to raise the sceptical questions than to produce the appropriate answers. One way of moving ahead will be to include some of the experiences gained over the last 30 years by practising some of Grundtvig's ideas in Third World countries, not least the Folk High School.

A Review of Earlier Initiatives

At the outset it is interesting to repeat that the initiatives to transfer the Folk High School idea were originally based on the assumption that the situation in the Third World was considered to be very much like 19th century Denmark, and for that reason it was essential to transfer "the experience of development" in 19th century Denmark to the "developing" world. Danish society had thrown off a foreign yoke, and following that newly won awareness there had been a political liberation of the oppressed groups, while at the same time ideals of democracy were realized and a high degree of social equality reached. The major force behind this process of change was thought to be Grundtvig's ideas as manifested first and foremost in the Folk High School movement. These schools would in the Third World countries become "counter-cultural" schools, and they would generate a development on the Danish or Scandinavian model. The method was to be the indirect one: the development of agriculture and other occupational sectors through the improvement of historical and cultural awareness.

One first observation is that it has been difficult to strike a balance between the school for life which was the main purpose, and general adult education with training in practical skills. Dr. Ozumba admits that he has had to compromise on Grundtvig's principle of having no examinations, and he tries to balance it with other measures, like the Grundtvig hour. It is also clear that in many places the emphasis has moved from consciousness-raising – the crucial factor in education for life – to training in skills needed in society. Various factors are behind this major shift in purpose and emphasis. One factor is that Folk High Schools in the Third World countries mainly cater for drop-outs, school leavers, suppressed groups like women. When the recruitment is done from such groups the demand for some officially recognized skills will naturally be high. Here we have the links between adult learning and vocational training which I touched upon earlier.

But the deviation from the original idea should probably be seen in a larger perspective. The Folk High School idea is transferred to societies where development is the main and almost the only item on the agenda, not a national awakening. Nor is it primarily a question of freedom from a foreign, imposed culture, but rather freedom from corruption and freedom from state intervention and government misuse of power. People's primary concern is the struggle to achieve better opportunities for the individual or possibly for the core family, but to a lesser degree for the whole community which the individuals belong to. Under these circumstances is it hardly realistic to imagine that the Folk High School idea will not be closely linked with the concept of development and thus geared to the current ideas of societal change which in turn means a strong emphasis on the acquierement of vocational skills and training. We may say that the Folk High School idea will easily turn into general adult education with which it originally was supposed to have nothing in common, at the expense of the so-called "awareness curriculum".

A second observation from the review of earlier initiatives has to do with the difficulty in coming to grips with what constitutes the unit which a common identity and a common sense of history should be based upon. We hear little about the nation as a separate cultural entity with its history and myths or about the use of a common language. On the contrary, the visible unit can hardly be the nation. In the case dealing with a Folk High School-like institution in Ghana much emphasis is put on the students' self-awareness generated by a strong emphasis on language, history and culture and by including local customs like storytelling, singing, and dancing. But the fellowship has been established on a purely tribal or ethnic basis which tends to cut off the wider unit, the nation state Ghana, and emphasize its heterogenous character. It is fully acknowledged that problems arise in relation to the history of Ghana and not least in relation to English which is the national language. But the limited local focus is so valuable in terms of the overall intention that in spite of it denouncing the concept of a nation, it has to take priority.

Here we are faced with a fundamental dilemma, first of all in Africa, the cleavage between the nation and the ethnic groups. When we talk about rediscovery of self and community, what kind of self and community are we referring to? Closest is the indigenous tradition found in the local context, but there is also the self and the community from the recent past "bastardized" as it is by colonialism and the so-called western civilization. From which of the available, but contradictory traditions should we develop our identity and our historical roots? Things are further complicated first by the religious pluralism which means that religion can hardly be a strong factor in strengthening common identity and fellowship, and secondly and even more pertinently the language situation with English as the medium of instruction, but not the mother tongue. Can a foreign language be the carrier of a common system of values? Or is it possible to generate Folkelighed in a language which is foreign to the people involved?

As quoted earlier Dr. Ozumba tends to answer in the negative as he is inclined to say that a Nigerian Folkelighed is hardly possible under these circumstances. This is probably the only conclusion to come to because on reflection the basic reality already touched upon is that in most Third World countries we cannot speak of nations as homogenous units carried by joint historical experiences and nourished by feelings of nationalism, but about political units more or less imposed from the outside and consisting of disparate group constituted according to ethnic and religious criteria. These are the conditions which democracy has to work on – the cleavage between people's primary loyalty and the nation.

The conclusion is that the usual vehicles or instruments for realizing Grundtvig's ideals cannot be used straight away in a Third World situation. It appears from most cases that in practice the nation is no longer the unit towards which the work of the Folk High Schools is geared. The schools appear to have settled for the ethnic or tribal basis and to relate the awareness curriculum to the traditions found at that level. But it has left them in a painful dilemma, and the hope is still one day to give the national dimension its proper place in the consciousness – raising activity of the Folk High Schools.

Grundtvig in a Third World Context: Adult Learning and a Democratic Awakening

The question to ask here is whether time has come to face the realities of this dilemma more directly and reach a higher level of clarification with regard to the possible transfer of Grundtvig's ideals and the Folk High School idea to a Third World situation. In recent years we have almost everywhere, and not only in the Third World, seen an upsurge of ethnic feelings which has made it difficult to use our usual terminology. Especially the distinction between nations and minorities has become difficult. What is one day considered to be an ethnically defined minority, has the next day been accepted as a nation in its own right. And all the feelings and expressions of a common identity which we normally associate with a nation are now reserved for the ethnic minorities, and their so to speak "national rights" have, to a large extent, been legitimized; national movements have become almost identical with ethnic movements.

At the same time the concept of the nation state which goes back to the 19th century is also in a process of change. It may not be as extreme as the former Jugoslavia which was said to consist of six mini-states, five ethnic groups, four languages, three religions and two alphabets. But especially in the Third World we have to reckon with nations that within their boundaries include a number of dichotomies which we did not use to associate with a nation: no identity between mother tongues and national language, no identity between religion and the nation and so on. Such situations give rise to questions which are almost unanswerable: when is a nation not a nation? And when is a minority a nation?

But they also lead us back to the point made earlier that essential elements in Grundtvig's ideals and in the Folk High School idea – like the necessary relationship between history, language and nation – are so rooted in a Danish context and presuppose a small nation with a common language, a joint historical tradition and a homogenous culture that they cannot just be transferred to other areas, not least to situations of great diversity which in many ways contradict these basic ideas.

Faced with such realities, while still convinced of the relevance of Grundtvig's ideas for many Third World countries, we can point to two ways ahead. The first one should simply be to reduce the dependency on Grundtvig's own very familiar categories of nation, language, mythology etc. So far the main criterion in judging the various activities has been how far they have functioned according to the original Folk High School idea and the basic principles first outlined by Grundtvig himself. After all, the basic message from Grundtvig as it is presented in the Folk High School idea does not stand or fall with his special vocabulary or with the special means he valued and suggested from his experiences.

This leads to the second suggestion. Without loosing the essence of Grundtvig's message and visions the attempt should be made to adjust Grundtvig's basic ideals and reformulate the original idea to face the prevailing circumstances and new challenges in the Third World. Instead of talking of a national awakening emphasis could be shifted towards a democratic awakening. Without dismissing the value of the identity rooted in culture and history the awareness of the idea of democracy could be just as important, not democracy as a system of government known in Europe, but as a way of living, as the principle guiding the relations between people, a principle that emphasizes responsibility and accountability in personal relations and also in the relationship between the ones who rule and the ones who are ruled. Such guidelines for people's attitudes and mutual relations could well be the objective of the socalled awareness-rising education or for the awareness curriculum associated with the Folk High School.

Concluding Remarks

Let me conclude by saying that faced with the challenge of gearing adult learning or adult education to the development of democracy it makes perfect sense to make use of Grundtvig's basic ideas and emphasize their universal value. But they have to be translated to meet the challenges facing us around the turn of a century. And they have to be lifted out of the special Danish historical context. What was the answer to the challenges faced by Danish society in the 19th century, will almost certainly not be the answer to the challenges of democracy facing us at the doorstep to the 21st century. The ultimate goal may be the same, but the means will have to be different. Adult learning is just as important if not more important in the present situation, and in that respect Grundtvig is as relevant as ever. But the methods to be employed have to take into account the situation prevailing in society. What worked well in another part of the world in a different age may not necessarily work under the present conditions. In this field we can learn from and be stimulated by history, but history should not be read in a fundamentalistic way.

Globalization, Internationalization, Regionalization: A Challenge for Adult Educators

Jorge Jeria

This article will explore some of the different ideas involved in the concept pf globalization, internationalization and regionalization. It will explore these concepts using a critical view of the human capital formation concept as the main driving force behind globalization, and the changes in education produced as a result of the globalization process. It will also try to articulate some form of coherent educational response.

Many educators responding to the economic internationalization and modernization have issued calls challenging educators for the need to respond to the political and economic internationalism in today's world which seems to be irreversible (Duke, C. 1994, Ilon 1995). At the same time this challenge calls to rethink the assymetrical relationship that is developed between technology, society and the economy of the countries. In other words it is indicated that the economic modernization and globalization have produced important changes, these changes have, however, produced further disparity, socially and economically. Thus, the role of education and adult education in particular is extremely important in recognizing these issues and providing avenues for responding to these changes.

The General Context of a Global Economy, Regionalization and Education

In order to discuss these issues it is important to reach some kind of agreement in terms of concept such as globalization, internationalization and regionalization. Globalization seems to be a term that is much in vogue today and is part of the increasing acceleration of global interdependence that we witness at different levels (Robertson, R. 1992). The term globalization in general is not new, since the emergence of international institutions and organizations prior to World War II predates the concept, however, the association with the nature of modernity is of recent development.

To this extent the debate has been in economic circles where internationalization ends and globalization begins or even the meaning associated with these terms. In some cases internationalization is referred to as to pertaining to the realm of multinational enterprises, and in other cases it is referred to nation-state policies. While the extent of the internationalization of the economy is true, it is also true that only the highly industrialized economies are the most involved and carry the banner of globalization (O'Hara-Devereaux & Johansen, R. 1994). Thus, one of the most important economic trends during the 1970s and 1980s has been the acceleration and interdependence between the sconomies of the highly industrialized countries (Gibbs and Michalak, 1994, Wilson, 1992).

Regionalization

A more recent trend seems to be the regionalization of the world economy. This has been a topic of much recent debate, in which education is by no means exempt, due to the implications and responses that are necessary in order to identify and attempt appropriate changes. Some authors have indicated that regionalization may further social inequality and claim that if regionalization is part of a "global system of economic exchanges, albeit advantaging groups differentially, then the education response must be systemic as well" (Ilon, L. 1994). Even further, the internationalization of the economy is argued, may provoke selections, discriminations, or educational categorization, which will exclude some people and advantage others (Gelpi, E. 1987).

The general context of regionalization is founded in the much larger idea of globalization and the results of the structural adjustment process. The movement of a country to a process of globalization usually passes through these structural adjustment policies, meaning "liberalization, deregulation, privatization and stabilization" (Ilon, 1995). Such is clearly the case of Mexico as an example which has been effected by decades of structural adjustment policies, being the expenditures for the education of one of the "hardest hit area" (Reimers, F. 1991). Some authors point out that regionalization can be interpreted as a result of "a set of policies that seek to regulate economic activity in a defined geographical area while at the same time reducing competition from outside competitors" (Michalak, 1994). Conceptualized this form it seems to be very close to the idea of the North American Free Trade Agreement (NAFTA) and the idea of the European Common Market (EEC) that seek to open the markets of the countries involved in order to fend for external competition from other regional markets. In the case of NAFTA the market to defend is in this case continental America, from the North to the South, under the increasing competition of Asian and European markets. At the same time this seems to be the response of the United States in particular to a decreased hegemonic role which is being balanced by a new view of the hemispheric role (Grinspun, R. and Cameron, M. 1993). As we understand in this paper the economic market has already developed its own strategies. Unfortunately, it needs to be seen to what extent this includes the response of education or what has been the response to the globalization process from educational circles.

Education

For the most part the relation of education to the above, can be summarized in two forms. The first assumption is taken from the point of view of a neo-classical human capital analysis, the expansion of economic markets in a global economy assumes that education is one of the driving forces behind the new path of economic development. The second assumption is taken from the point of view of a societal modernization theory which makes reference mainly to those measurable attributes found in society, such as: education, occupation, literacy, income and wealth. It does not deal with for example culture, democracy and other similar attributes as these are considered unmeasurable. The two earlier assumptions are linked to the notion of economic development and modernization and the rational allocation of resources found in the human capital theory. Using the first two assumptions we find that recent debates about work and education and some policy making decisions make use of these ideas to demonstrate that the changing nature of jobs as a result of its globalization and internationalization, increasing competition and technological demands imply further education (Ilon, 1994, US Department of Education, 1994, Minister of Employment and Immigration, Canada, 1984). One of the implications of this assumption is that a better education will allow for better competitiveness and productivity; therefore a better education will equal a good worker (Pines and Carnevale, 1991). From this perspective, it is also implied that in order to achieve these goals it is necessary to change and reform the schools in order to keep them in line with the changing nature of the marketplace. National policies of education which emanated from centralized ministries of education are now transformed in local policies, and schools are managed at local levels in order to provide the necessary flexibility to supply the global market. An example of these policies that radically changed schooling from national policies to local level policies and school decentralization is the case of Chile (Carnoy, M. 1995) and lately Mexico (Calvo Ponton, 1996). Not many results are yet available about this decentralization process, however, we find that some international agencies

UNESCO, UNICEF have issued a call for equity and quality and "education for all". What we know is that education has been provided unequally and those without economic resources are unable to compete in a system of human capital formation. One of the unintended results of these policies for the governments is that when they adjust their structures and their economies to a larger, global scale, their national boundaries are less demarcated. In the past governments the main promoters of national identity were through education, this is no longer possible since education in this context means to compete globally. On the other hand, those unable to compete will be left out to let their community find available resourses. Last, for those who are globally employable nearly any country will open its dors.

Associated with this is the idea that education and learning are continuous, does not end with formal education and that adults will need to be engaged in this continuous learning process as long as they are employed or unemployed. This perspective indicates to us that a person will have to spread out his/her educational experiences according to the emerging needs in his/her working life (Carnoy, M. and Levin, H. 1985) in order to accomodate him/herself to the market. Translated into economic terms this means to be flexible. Thus, participating in formal education and training throughout life in order to maintain a job and the flexibility of the occupation lend credibility to the notion that a more educated workforce will in turn result in higher productivity. At the same time, studies in participation in recurrent, continuing education programs indicate that those taking advantage of these programs tend to be those who are highly educated and occupy higher occupational positions (Carnoy, M. and Levin, H. 1985, Cross, P. 1981, Quigley, A. 1990). Of course this group is small, but in terms of influence over policy direction their actions are large. As a result a potential gap is created in terms of education and income in which those with a more formal education tend to seek more, while those left behind will have a more difficult time finding employment, thus creating further marginalization and in other cases discrimination (Carnoy, M., Daley, H., Hinojosa, R. 1993, Rubenson, K. 1987).

The neo-classical assumption of the use of adult continuing education and training considers it to be essential to maintain what is "considered a quality workforce" (Hornbeck, 1994) which will be able to compete for business and to participate in international labor markets.

Labor markets which have become competitive, flexible and decentralized in an era of the new post-fordism allow for a continuous process of education and training, while at the same time building social inequality. In this case continuing education represents a commodity that allows for greater flexibility as in business.

Conclusion

From the perspective of human capital formation competitive advantages today make raw materials and industrial production possible worldwide, making economic gains minimal as competition globalizes. Highly skilled and channeled human resources, however, take long term investment, it requires careful planning, needs to be of high quality and is potentially a resource unmatched for economic growth.

Perhaps more daunting is the notion that benefits to be derived from the human resource explosion, will not benefit all. In fact, the globalization of the economy will mean that many people become even more marginal, this "education for all" may also mean marginalization for many.

In this case, the task of adult educators is of extreme importance. A Critical analysis of current trends at local and global scales may allow for a better understanding of current trends. The "unmeasurable attributes" such as democratization, culture and human rights need to become an essential element in any educational context.

Bibliography

Carnoy, M. (1995): *Is School Privatization the Answer?* Education Week Vol. XIV, 40 pp 52-40

Carnoy, M., Daley, H., Hinojosa O. R. (1994): The Changing Economic Position of Latinos in the US Labor Market since 1939. In *Latinos in a Changing US Economy* ed. by Morales, R. and Bonilla, F. Newbury Park, CA: Sage

Carnoy, M., Levin, H. M. (1985): *Schooling and Work in the Democratic State.* Stanford CA; Stanford University Press

Calvo Ponton, B. (1996): *"Education Policy and the Mexican Project for Modernizing Basic Education".* Paper presented at the meeting of the Society for Comparative end International Education, Boston MA 1995

Cross, C. (1981): *Adults as Learners: Increasing Participation and Facilitating Learning.* San Fransisco: Josses Bass

Duke, C. (1994): *"Trends in the development of adult education as a profession".* Adult Education and Development. Institute for International Cooperation of the German Adult Education Association, No. 43

Gelpi, E. (1987): Education, Production, Development and Technological Innovation. In Leirman W. and Kulich J. ed. *Adult Education and the Challenges of the 1990s.* N. Y.: Croom Helm

Grinspun, R. and Cameron, M. (1993): The Political Economy of North American Integration: Diverse Perspectives, Converging Criticism. In Grinspun, R. and Cameron, M. ed. *The Political Economy of the North American Free Trade.* New York: St. Martin Press

Hornbeck, D. (1991): New Paradigms for Action. In *Human Capital and America's Future.* ed. by Hornbeck, D. and Salamon, L. Baltimore and London: The J. Hopkins University Press

Ilon, L. (1994): *Structural adjustment and education: adapting to a growing global market.* International Journal of Educational Development. Vol. 14, No. 2

Michalak, W. (1994): The Political economy of trading blocks. In *Continental trading blocks: The Grow of Regionalism in the World Economy.* ed. by Gibb, R. and Michalak, W. New York: J. Wiley and Sons Ltd.

Ministry Employment and Immigration (1984) Consultation Paper: Training. Ottawa: Department of Supply and Services

O'Hara-Devereaux, M. and Johansen, R. (1994): *Globalwork.* San Fransisco: Jossie Bass

Pines, M. and Carnevale, A. (1991): Employment and training. In *Human Capital and America's Future.* ed. by Hornbeck, D. and Salamon, L. Baltimore and London: The J. Hopkins University Press

Quigley, A. B. (1990): *"Hidden Logic: Reproduction and Resistance in Adult Literacy and Adult Basic Education".* Adult Education Quarterly. V. 40 (2) pp. 103-115

Reimers, F. (1991): *The Impact of Economic Stabilization and Adjustment on Education in Latin America.* Comparative Education Review, Vol. 35, No. 2

Robertson, R. (1992): *Globalization, Social Theory and Global Culture.* London: Sage

Rubenson, K. (1987): Adult Education: The economic context. In *Choosing our Future.* ed. by Cassidy, F. and Faris, R. Toronto: Ontario Institute for Studies in Education

U. S. Department Education (1994): *"Building a Nation of Leaders"* National Educational Goals Panel. The National Educational Goals Dpt. Washington D. C.

Wilson, P. (1992): *Exports and Local Development. Mexico's New Maquiladoras.* Austin: University of Texas Press

Repair, Defend, Invent: Civil Societarian Adult Education Faces the Twenty-First Century

Michael R. Welton

I: Epochal Development?

There is a lot of despair around, no doubt about it – Jean-François Lyotard (1984) has observed that the 20th century has given us as "much terror as we can take". Eric Hobsbawm's recent essay "Barbarism: A User's Guide" (1994) argues that there has been a profound disruption and breakdown of the systems of rules and moral behaviour by which all societies regulate the relations between their members and those of other societies. He thinks that the project of the 18th century enlightenment – the establishment of universal rules and standards of moral behaviour – has reversed, and we are descending into barbarism... into darkness. We scan the globe and mourn for those "disintegral nations" like Bosnia, Sri Lanka or Rwanda that reenact the "horrors of the ancient slaughter-house" (Barber, 1995).

At the other extreme, the "end of history" ideologies, captured in Francis Fukuyama's work, The End of History and the Last Man (1992). This book is a celebration of the final triumph of liberal democracy and the "free market" in our increasingly intertwined and homogenized world. History, in the Hegelian sense, has come to an end in its great, unifying synthesis. The world is becoming more democratic – have no fear! But there is a lot to fear, I'm afraid. Police truncheons continue to crack heads open, from Indonesia to Paris. Yes Fukuyama's utopianism does capture a moment of truth as we lurch towards the 21st century.

I want to argue for a modest and chastened utopianism as we face the new millennium.

- Chastened because we have learned that political projects that seek to totally remake the world and humankind have radiated nothing but disaster (Now we must speak of the self-limiting nature of transformative ideals

- Modestly utopian because the dissolution of communism and the crisis of the welfare-state – both losing their capacity to mobilize for an alternative future – provide us with an "unprecedented historical opportunity to rethink the structural possibilities for the democratization of modern societies" (Wolin, 1993, p. 576).

My argument, posed for consideration towards the UNESCO meeting in Hamburg, Germany in 1997, is that of a new self-understanding of the transformative potential of late modern societies hinges on the rediscovered and reinvigorated concept of civil society. The concept of civil society, on the tip of many people's tongues, has an ancient pedigree. But its contemporary revival exploded into our sensibilities with the "civil society against the state" movement in Eastern Europe. Since then, consideration of civil society has been taken up by NGO activists, academics, and many others. It is as if the air we breathe, that sustains us, that makes all the plenitude of human activity possible, is no longer taken-for-granted. We most surely live in a "risk society" (Ulrich Beck), and there is a widespread sense, throughout the globe, that the current global economic restructuring poses great threats to the moral, spiritual and social bases for living well with one another.

II: Changing Configurations

It seems to me that the main cause of much of the disorder and confusion within most societies (and the global adult education movement) has to do with the changing configuration of the relationship between economy, the state and civil society. The "economy" has pried itself loose from the constraining effects of the "state", and has turned a deaf ear to the agonies reverberating through civil society and the life histories of men and women. Systemic deficiencies, we should never tire of reminding ourselves, are always experienced in the context of individual life histories. The language of economy, money and market has colonized our public vocabularies (maybe even our private), displacing spiritual, moral and social-critical vocabularies. The fundamental strategy of the "new right" has been to emasculate the signifiers of culture by attributing to them denuded economic meanings. "Freedom" becomes absence of "economic restraint", "equality" the opportunity to compete, and "efficiency" becomes the master signifier of the new right by elevating itself to an end-in-itself. Why has the adult and higher education community been so unable to resist marketspeak?

We speak glowingly of finance capital, of physical capital and even human capital. Rarely do we speak of social capital. But this is changing as we become aware of the way global restructuring is depleting relations of mutuality and trust within our associational lives. The American sociologist, Robert Putnam, defines social capital as the "processes between people which establish networks, norms and social trust and faciliate co-ordination and cooperation for mutual benefit" (Cox, 1995, p. 15). And it is precisely within the domain of what we are now calling civil society (the social space which includes intimate relationships, friendship, associations, social movements and public spheres) that social capital is produced or depleted. While social capital is only one of the core components of a vitally functioning civil society (the institutions and learning processes of civil society also have the normative task of producing meaning and critically active personalities), if relationships of trust and reciprocity are damaged one can scarcely imagine life making much sense or persons functioning in stable fashion. The unspeakable tragedy (is that the right word?) of Rwanda illustrates the madness that humans can descend into when trust is striped from all interactions.

Relationships of mutuality, reciprocity and trust, when they occur, are carefully nurtured over time. Social capital is analogous to the growth of an oak tree. It starts out precariously as an acorn, then a small shoot, facing wind, cold, animals. Over a hundred years or so, it reaches its full sturdiness. In a matter of minutes, modern technology can burst it on this tree and destroy it. Social capital is like that: it takes years of care and nurturance to foster meaningful relationships of respect and tolerance. And the heedless action of the state or corporation can destroy accumulated social capital (in those societies where civil society has emerged with some autonomy and strength) almost over night. Stockholders are told that profits have soared in the same breath as we are informed that the company has been downsized. Decisions made only in terms of economic efficiency neglect the pain that reaches into the human psyshe and does not notice the fault-lines that appear in our families and associations, let alone the almost unbearable pressures exerted on the overstressed welfare state. Australian Eva Cox comments: "Social capital should be the pre-eminent and most valued form of capital as it provides the basis on which we build a truly civil society. Without our social bases we cannot be fully human. Social capital is as vital as language for human society. We become vulnerable to social bankruptcy when our social connections fail. If most of our experiences enhance our sense of trust and mutuality, allowing us to feel valued and to value others, then social capital increases" (1995, p. 17).

These insights ought to provide some encouragement for beleaguered socially responsible adult educators. The "education for social transformation" discourse, with its orientation to strategic action to change the way people think and institutions perform, may obscure the way our educational practice (in and out of classrooms) either produces or depletes social capital. The global adult education movement must consider the extent to which its practices conserve and sustain the social basis for what Habermas has called communicative action. Socially responsible adult education (SRAE) is not simply about "social change". In fact, one could make a strong case that SRAE must grapple as never before with the following learning challenges engendered by globalization: the deprivation of meaning (which confronts consumerism as surrogate god), the depletion of solidarity (which confronts possessive individualism and social fragmentation) and the destabilization of the personality (which confronts many pathologizing tendencies in our world). In our topsy-turvy world, SRAE may well emerge as "philosophic conservatism", defined by Anthony Giddens as a "philosophy of protection, conservation and solidarity..." He thinks that a "radical political programme must recognize that confronting manufactured risk cannot take the form of "more of the same', an endless exploration of the future at the cost of protection of the present or past" (1994, p. 10).

I believe that a new self-understanding of society at the end of the 20th century is emerging from the rubble and ruins of past-communist and post-welfare societies as well as the unspeakable suffering and misery of millions of people living in societies that lack traditions of liberal rights and vital publics. Indeed, as one person commented to me after a talk on "civil society", "I think that civil society is just a perk of the affluent countries. Our attention ought to be elsewhere, namely, on the transnational corporations that rule everyone". Well, I don't believe that the transnational corporations do rule everything even though they certainly are responsible for bad things. And if a "Third World" country lacks an open civil society, then this has to be grappled with in terms of the future of democracy. For me, our attention as SRAE must be on strengthening our capacity to react to the colonization of our lifeworlds.

III: Civil Society as the Natural Habitat of SRAE

As an adult learning theorist (at least these are my pretensions), I have increasingly come to realize that civil society is the privileged domain for non-instrumental learning processes. This is a normative statement; of course, actually existing relationships within civil society can be destructive or manipulative. This is why Habermas uses the phrase "rationalized lifeworld" to capture both the possibility of pathologies within the lifeworld and the necessity of persons arriving at norms, values and procedures that govern their interactions through reflexive, deliberative learning processes. Communication within the institutions of civil society is oriented to understanding, and we recognize, both intuitively and rationally, that when a spouse, for instance, coerces a partner into a particular act through force, this is a distortion of what ought to be mutually agreed upon.

The institutions of civil society, which have evolved over time in interplay with the development of complex sub-systems of state and economy (an important rule-of-thumb here is that learning and action within the sub-systems tends to be governed by strategic intentions, and that learning and action within civil society tends to be governed by communicative intentions), have the task of enabling us to learn what life means, who we are, what holds us together, what divides us and what it means to be competent, active persons in our particular world. In sociological language, we can speak of the cultural, social and personal reproductive tasks of civil society. This rather flat language does not fully indicate quite what is at stake. If the reproductive tasks are interfered with, or cannot be carried out for systemically-rooted reasons, then the very spiritual, moral and social infrastructure of the "economy" and "state" will be imperiled. And, it is precisely this infrastructure that is being damaged in the current economic restructuring. Global SRAE has the opportunity at this critical historical juncture to re/assert a humanist, life-affirming language against the life-denying language of economics. A message scrawled on a wall in the suburbs of Melbourne, Australia – "Death to Economics, Viva Humanity!" captures something of this truth.

I would like to argue that the core value structure of socially responsible adult education – the affirmation that the lifeworld is the foundation of meaning, solidarity and stable personality; that our commitment to the enlightened, relatively autonomous and reflective learner; to the centrality of social learning processes to the formation of the active citizen; and to the fostering of discussion, debate and dialogue amongst citizens – it is compatible with "discursive" or "deliberative" approaches to democracy. And "civil society" – the normative realm of communicative action and self-organization – is the key to understanding the meaning of deliberate democracy.

The Association of World Education has its task the preparation documents addressing the issue of Adult Education, citizenship and democracy. The matter of adult education and citizenship is very complex, and requires elaborated and many-faceted discussion. But I believe that a civil societarian approach to these questions holds some promise towards understanding how global adult education can contribute to the further democratization of societies in the

North and South. Three axioms emerge from the extensive literature on civil society that are pertinent to our discussion. First, the scope and vitality of a society's associational life is a prerequisite for building a deliberate democracy. We learn to be citizens, not by participating in "politics" first, but in the "free spaces" of school, church, clubs and associations. Associations are "schools of citizenship": in these associations men and women learn to respect and trust others, fulfill obligations and press their claims communicatively.

Second, in modern societies the new social movements take on a special significance as action-oriented sites for learning democracy. Movements like peace, ecology, women, indigenous peoples' struggles, etc. are certainly bound up with identity-assertion. But the learning processes inside the movements are oriented to bringing up issues relevant to the entire society, defining ways of approaching problems, proposing possible solutions, supplying new information and interpreting values differently and mobilizing good reasons and criticizing bad ones (Habermas 1996, p. 370).

Third, the creation and maintenance of exuberant public spheres is central to civil societarian adult education. Parkin maintains that the "Public sphere and civil society are not identical; rather, the public sphere is a central element of civil society in that it is via the institutions of the public sphere that members of civil society can engage in informed public debate upon matters of common concern, including the way in which power is distributed and deployed within society" (1995, p. 3). A dynamic and vigorous public sphere depends on the "favourable organization of civil society" (Calhoun, 1993, p. 276). For it is in the learning life of associations, organizations and movements that systemically generated problems, which reverberate first in individual life histories, are distilled and transmitted in "amplified form to the public sphere" (Habermas, 1996, p. 367). The public sphere is, of course, not an identifiable thing-in-itself. A geographical area within a city, for example, may function primarily as a park for picnickers and the sportsminded. It may also become a public space for a rally or protest against state or corporate actions. I believe that the new social movements often play particularly salient roles, in late modernity, in ensuring that reflective learning processes occur outside the control of government and private corporate interests. But it is not just the new social movements that assume this role. Any association, even if it is usually not-"political", can under certain circumstances, attempt to gain public attention and foster widespread debate around an issue of major concern to citizens. For instance, a bird-watching society (which fosters learning processes related to birds and their environment) may be galvanized into collective action when it notices that a particular species has not been seen as much as usual.

Indeed, this learning process could result in the major identification of a serious ecological problem. The bird-watching club, however, would have to get the public's attention, and mobilize the public through various adult education initiatives in order to influence political decision makers.

Civil societarian adult educators would be committed, I believe, to a process of double democratization. The principle that the division between the state and civil society must be a central feature of democratic life is fundamental to this outlook on societal learning processes. The second premise must be that the power to make desicions be free of the inequalities and constraints that can be imposed by an unregulated system of capital (Held, 1993). This means that the learning processes within civil society – the organization of enlightenment in Habermas's terms – are oriented towards the generating of influence through the "life of democratic associations and unconstrained discussion in the cultural public sphere" (Cohen and Arato, 1992). SRAE would decry any form of democracy that focused on voting while confining citizen action largely to the "private" sidelines of civil society. There must be institutionalized opportunities to exist and act as citizens, as participants in public life. With reference to the history of Canadian adult education, I have argued that institutions like the Citizen's and Farm Radio Forums of the 1940s and 1950s were seminal attempts to institutionalize social and political learning processes in order to channel influence from the lifeworld to the system. Without active participation on the part of citizens in egalitarian institutions and civil associations as well as "politically relevant" organizations, there will be no way to maintain the democratic character of any society.

We have learned some big lessons as the 20th century comes to a close. The old leftist dream of bringing society as a whole under control lies in ruins. Civil societarian adult educators must learn lessons from the "civil society against the state" struggles of Eastern Europe that any viable project for the further democratization of society must be self-limiting. We cannot abolish the "state" or the "market". Habermas argues that "democratic movements emerging from civil society must give up holistic aspirations to a self-organizing society, aspirations that also undergirded Marxist ideas of social revolution. Civil society can directly transform only itself, and it can have at most an indirect effect on the selftransformation of the political system; generally, it has an influence only on the personnel and programming of this system" (1996, p. 372). But the self-limitation of civil society should not be understood as incapacitation or paralysis. Civil society, Habermas reminds us, has the "opportunity of mobilizing counterknowledge and drawing on the pertinent forms of expertise to make its own translations" (1996, p. 372). Thus, it becomes very important to understand the circumstances under which civil society can acquire influence in the public sphere and have an effest on the parliamentary complex (and the courts) through its own public opinions and compel the political (or economic) systems to open itself to learning emerging from civil society. Collective learning processes, emerging within civil society, must have their crystallized demands channeled through the gates and into the arenas of formal decision-making (within state and economic subsystems). Do socially responsible adult educators understand how this works? Most assuredly, the global adult education movement must deepen its theoretical understanding of the circumstances under which a mobilized civil society is able to find receptors for its concerns within the system-domains.

In conclusion, I think that any vital socially responsible adult education in the 21st century must face this question: how can civil society be secured, sustained and invigorated in our time? A strong civil society is prerequisite for the creation of any kind of vital (or even efficient) democratic society. We are presently enslaved to an anti-public, anti-human way of seeing and ordering the world. Therefore:

- a rational, dynamic, mobilized, exuberant civil society must be defended where it has emerged

- repaired where the system has damaged it, and

- invented where tyrannical states have strangled it.

Socially responsible adult education, at the cusp of the 21st century, has its fundamental purpose, the strengthening, defending, and expanding of the scope and inclusiveness of civil society – to help to tilt the balance of power away from government, bureaucracies, and privately-owned corporations, in favour of individuals and independent public associations active within civil society (Parkin, 1995, pp. 17-18).

Biography

Barber, J., Jihad vs. McWorld. NY: Random House, 1995

Calhoun, C.: *Civil Society and the Public Sphere*. Public Culture, 5, 193

Cohen, J. and Arato, A.: *Civil Society and Political Theory*. Cambridge: Mass. 1992

Cox, Eva: *A Truly Civil Society*. Sydney: Australian Broadcast Corporation, 1995

Giddens, A.: *Beyond Left and Right: The Future of Radical Politics*. Stanford: Stanford University Press, 1994

Habermas, J.: *Between Facts and Norms: Contributions to a Discourse Theory of Law and Democracy*. Cambridge: MIT Press, 1996

Held, D.: *Liberalism, Marxism and Democracy*. Theory and Society, 22, 1993

Hobsbawm, E.: *Barbarism: a user's guide*. New Left Revies, 206, July-August 1994

Lyotard, Jean-François: *The Postmodern Condition*. Minneapolis: University of Minnesota Press, 1984

Wolin, R.: *Review of Cohen and Arato* (1992). Theory and Society, 22, 1993

Adult Education Facing the Hungarian and the Central-European Challenges

Judit Rónai

Let me begin by telling you a little bit about the sources that I drew upon for the information I wish to share with you in this article.

The most fundamental source of it is my own life experience. The time and place of my birth and life and my life experience in the processes of change that have taken place. During this time, through my life experiences, the world has become more and more universal for me.

My life is closely connected with the place which is my homeland. I am talking about a location of dramatic events, a location where in the course of history people have always had to face fundamental challenges concerning the issues of being Hungarian as well as European, being simple folks as well as universal in the embrace of geographical, historical and cultural forces.

Local people expressed their reaction to these challenges in various activities and ways of behaviour which resulted in the town being awarded the title "the Most Faithful Hungarian Town" and gained distinction and respect in the whole region.

And you all know that this is the historic place, where the iron curtain was first broken through what was a clear fact that a new world situation had come about.

Through the common research with international institutions, through the Association for World Education and through the deeper and deeper knowledge of the situation and the mission of the United Nations and UNESCO I have obtained valuable sources from which to draw upon. I am convinced that these international organizations will have a growing importance in the future, however, the success of their endeavors in the struggle to ground an active and moral citizenship in the world cannot be realized without the cooperation of competent international non-governmental organizations.

I do hope that the Central-European Folk Academy as part of our common strategy will have a significant role in our struggle for a living, peaceful and secure world.

My task is to impart to you the Hungarian and Central European situation from the aspects of a Global point of view. Here I have to mention a marvelous source for my chosen task. There was a recent conference organized by the Future Research Committee of the Hungarian Academy of Sciences. The theme of this conference was "Hungary on the Threshold of the Twenty-first Century". I have to express my heartfelt gratitude to be able to have this material for my own reference and for sharing some of the important ideas that fit into our responsibilities here.

According to this Conference the vision of the world has been dominated in a way which was Europe-centred for the past five centuries: the security of Europe has had a central place in the international system of the history of security. Until 1945 the security of Europe was defined by an effort to reach a balance of power as a resultant of the correlation between interests and counter interests.

Events during World War II, however, indicated and sped up processes which led to the transformation of Europe's security: a dominant security system changed into a security system of secondary importance. Thus Europe lost its control and autonomy over the status and dynamism of its own security system.

So one of the most important consequences of the war, in regards to security systems, was the breaking of this long period, even in a historical sense, which was characterized by a very close correlation between European and international interests of security which were determined by Europe.

The period between 1945 and 1989 was dominated by the superpowers, so much that European security as a unit based on the system of correlation of the European countries ceased to exist. Instead of this, the fate of European security was defined by the global rivalry between the two superpowers.

A metamorphosis of the security system started in 1989, and with the re-arrangement of the power relations new hazards and destabilizing factors have shaped the political map of Europe.

These processes started from Eastern Europe and from the successor states of the former Soviet Union and created a division at an enormous speed. The system of conditions for security can hardly be seen, and is perhaps even further away from stabilization and from the consolidation of the system than it was in 1989 when "the revolution of the East" swept through the region. The traditionally existing and inherited destabilizing forces in the region were only in a deep-frozen state during the cold war just waiting to be revitalized when the pressure forced on them by external forces ceased to exist. The policy of great powers also stifled the efforts to create nationalistic states in Central Eastern Europe so that these efforts erupted with elementary force when the grip eased off. Historically this process took place parallel with the appearance of crisis situations penetrating through the great power centres of the world.

Thus the economic and political destabilization of Eastern Europe has a dual source: from the aggravation of fate-like crises processes in Eastern Europe and from the general defenselessness from global trends which have an impact on the whole of the world economy.

What are the global processes; the maturation of which must be taken into account in the 90's and which have a significant influence on the security of the world and thus on the security of Eastern Europe as well?

The role of economic potential and economic links has undergone fundamental revaluation mainly because of the fact that the philosophy of nuclear deterrent has become meaningless. Economic power is more and more becoming a strategic factor in international relations and in guaranteeing the security of the world.

At the same time economic policy or various trends in economic policy which were thought to be omnipotent for decades proved to be a complete failure. Neither restrictive monetarism, nor Keynesianism with the aim to enhance demand could provide anything new in the transformed situation of the world economy. On the other hand no new, coherent economic philosophy has been created. So we must face a historical paradox: in a period of the absolute revaluation of the elements of economic security the world economy can be characterized fundamentally by a decrease in growth.

This process has been going on for some years now. If we analyze the situation of the global processes which have a fundamental influence on the development of economic power centres in the world, it becomes clear that the expected economic boom in the USA did not take place, the deteriorating output in the economy of Japan has become almost palpable, Western Europe has shown serious decay in a period when serious growth impulses were expected from the Maastricht Treaty which came into effect. The output in the Baltic countries and Russian has fallen dramatically, and with contradictory Poland recession continued in each eastern European country.

The world economy has really been shaken by a model crisis. And while on the one hand the economy of the world is moving towards globalization, on the other, the different character model crisis of regions might result in the inharmonious ability of certain regions of world economy and strengthens regionalization trends against globalization.

How can these world economic trends be imaged for Eastern Europe, and what are the processes that caused the internal, autonomous crises in the economies of Eastern Europe?

The "revolution of the east" which took place within the boundaries of the nationalistic states raised the false illusion that these countries would be able to get rid of the serious double heritage of the ambiguous civilian revolutions and the 40 years of social development at the same time, and that they would be able to build a socialist market economy based on parliamentary democracy.

The political and economic crisis in central and eastern Europe also bears signs of a model crisis. The monetary policy to stop the deterioration in the capacity of the economies and the earlier generally accepted economic philosophy to handle the debt crisis did not only prove unsuitable, but has launched dramatic external and internal indebtedness, accelerated the outflux of resources, and the parallel restrictive policy has led to a catastrophic deterioration of the productive sector.

Changing Configurations and Civil Society

In the former communist countries instead of only capital generation the re-allocation of capital has taken place thus dividing the middle classes which are weak anyway. So the precondition for the formulation of a civil society, the existence of a strong middle class can also be outlined in the distant future. Instead of the economic development, which has caused serious disappointment, the political leadership has concentrated on political solutions almost everywhere in the hope of success.

In a social sense such a large scale of polarization has been created that it has had a negative influence on civil development. The order of values of civil societies could not be transferred to this region. The objective is a civil society without middle classes and civil values.

So the conversion to a stable market economy which can develop cannot be realized in the absence of the three significant preconditions: there are no stable and strong middle classes, inequality in society is too high and a strong state with incentive intervention is missing. These factors strongly question the stability of existing structures and the chances of a democratic transition.

In the system of conditions for security in Eastern Europe the hazard factors are not of military nature, they are rather of an economic, social, ethnical and natural-environmental origin.

The differences in the level of the national economies will result in destabilizing processes which will be manifested on an international economic level.

There is imbalance in the region as a result of the fact that in spite of the balancing mechanism of the former COMECON certain differences have remained because of the original differences in the economic development which will only grow during the period of conversion to a market economy.

Links with the world economy, links with developed countries which might be converted into development potential might play a decisive part in the improvement of the internal conditions of the development of the national economies so that they can close the gap between themselves and the world economy. This is why it is understandable that tension in economic and trade conflicts is growing. Rivalry for aid and loans, the race for international capital might also result in further tension. The global lack of capital forecast for the 1990's might even accelerate the race for capital since the utilization of foreign capital in the former Communist countries is an essential tool so that these countries can close the gap between themselves and the world economy.

The uneven development in the countries of the region, the widening gap between East and West can induce a new wave of refugee migration thus can further deteriorate relationships among these countries in the region. All this has a multiple impact on Eastern Europe.

All of this seems to justify the fact that if a political culture follows the path of nationalism, it finds the way to pluralism and tolerance with enormous difficulty.

The efforts to regulate the destabilizing processes which appear on the level of nationalistic states and on a regional level take place parallel with the process of model crisis emanating from the large power centres of the world economy towards which Europe is by far defenseless. Thus the strengthening regionalism, in other words protectionism does not create the world economic driving environment which might help Central Eastern Europe through the difficulties of modernization.

In reality Eastern Europe has to face the question of whether it is possible to perform successful transformation on the periphery of the capitalistic world economy which is in crisis itself. A fundamental transformation, which, after independence is gained and modernization carried out, with social security and peace would introduce the period of freedom and pluralism (democracy).

The question must be asked in Eastern Europe again: is there an opportunity for a break out for each country on the eastern side of Europe, form a type of development pushed into the peripheries historically? Is there a chance for catching up, for a shift towards equal chances? Or the situation that has always characterized the flexibility of the West, the situation of asymmetric reciprocity will remain: The national revenues of the peripheries will be pumped to the west. Will the century-old practice prevail that "the resource of the wellbeing of the centre is the backwardness of the periphery?"

The above analysis is based on the research work of Judit Balázs, the famous Hungarian economist, who is at the same time the president of the European Peace Research Association. She summerises the process in the following way.

According to the analysis of the region east of the river Elba has become a crisis region after the disintegration of the bipolar world order. Most of the present day conflicts seem to be unsoluble at least in the short run. Objective difficulties are made more serious by subjective mistakes. The deterioration of the economies and the social tensions are shifting these countries towards new historical cul de sacs. A disintegrating Eastern Europe is looking for a path towards a strongly integrated Western Europe as a buffer zone between East and West thus providing defense for the West against the dramatic consequences resulting from the disintegration of the former Soviet Union.

Eastern Europe suffering from a lack of security today can step over the shadow of its past only slowly and through serious conflicts and can then create the security of the region. This will in all probability be a long and painful process, and in the meantime there will be a lot of crises in the development of Eastern Europe. The formulation of a new world order is an inevitable consequence of all this since the shift towards symmetric reciprocity today is not prompted by humanitarian reasons, but by economic necessity. Within the framework of the existing world order the economies forced into the periphery of the large power centres mean a diminishing revenue and, on the other hand they will pose as a growing hazard source for the richer regions of the world. The first step of this shift could be the elimination of this vicious circle the arrangement of the enormous state debts. IF THE CREATION OF A REASONABLE NEW ORDER IS NOT SUCCESSFUL, THE TURN OF THE CENTURY WILL BE ACCOMPANIED BY NEW TYPES OF WARS, A MODERN MIGRATION OF NATIONS, "ETHNIC CLEANSING", AND A WAVE OF VIOLENCE MOTIVATED BY HATRED.

Rudolph Andorka, a famous Hungarian sociologist, stated that his sociological research over the past few decades and of the present day situation led him to the conclusion that the most serious challenge facing Hungarian society is not only the poor state of the economy, but the lack of consensus of values and norms and the lack of practice within a democratic culture necessary for the operation of a developed market economy and political democracy, in other words, the greatest challenge is the struggle against anomy and alienation.

Adult Education and Democracy

In connection with the above statement I have to mention the great debate over a new constitution that is now occurring in the Hungarian Parliament. The most exciting question about the new constitution from our point of view is whether or not it will help the functioning of a participatory or representative democracy. This situation reflects the extent of the challenges described by Rudolph Andorka and the need to overcome apathy and alienation. Adult education has a great importance in the influencing of this situation because it is of global interest not to let unintegrated societies into the global democratic process.

I am convinced that this is not solely a challenge for Hungarian Society but one of global proportions. The challenge is how to motivate people for an active, creative and responsible life in an age when consumerism in the West and poverty in the East imprison people into a passive position. The new challenge truly lies in the search for the techniques of participatory democracy. These techniques must then be launched into democratic culture. Here I have the pleasure to mention the idea of a famous, Hungarian author, Gyula Hernády who suggests that in the important questions of a country or society members of the local governments should have a responsibility in the decision making process together with members of the parliament. I think that in this way local societies and individuals could be more actively and directly involved in the decision making process.

We must all take the above analysis very seriously for the very simple, historical fact that two world wars began within the Central European Region.

Isn't it a part of the world where ADULT EDUCATION has a real misson for a hopeful future?

Changes in the Global Judical Conception

Is a New World-Law Being Created From Below Because of the Formation of Numerous International Ties Between People and Organizations?

Hanne Petersen

Until the end of the 15th century it was the predominant belief in Europe that the world was flat – like a pancake. When you reached the boundaries of the pancake you risked falling into the bottomless abyss.

This picture of the world was at the same time geo-centric and teo-centric. The earth was the center of the universe and God was the highest authority. That is why it took the Catholic Church several hundred years to sanction the conception of the world which was the result of Galileo's research and the explorations, namely that the world is not flat but round.

The western jurisprudence is still – in a way – operating on the assumption that the world is flat. In the historical sense modern jurisprudence has had the nation state as a basis and perhaps also as a project.

The nation state was a geographically bound unity with a well defined center. After secularization and democratization this was no longer a feudal or religious center, but a temporal, political center.

At the top of democracy was the almost mythical law-maker who was second to none. Outside the boundaries was judicial nothingness, or at least the aliens, the barbarians, the savages.

The question is if the legal conception of the world is changing and is about to realize that the world is no longer flat, but actually round. In a ball or in a globe the center is in the middle. The outside of the ball is surface and periphery in relation to the inner center. The surface of the earth – or periphery – is interrelated with countless ties and currents. Air routes, radio waves, satellites, telecommunication, air currents and sea currents connect the remotest parts with each other in the course of still shorter periods of time. These ties and currents create patterns and links which become more evident when the perspectives are no longer viewed from the center of the earlier pancakes.

Looking at the globe from space with changing perspectives one will observe new and hitherto unacknowledged interrelations. These mutual ties bring forward connections, experiences, information, export-possibilities, and communication-possibilities of a hitherto unknown kind and magnitude. And they bring refugees, pollution and fear of the consequences of the collapse of the old order.

But regardless of how much Europe tries with Schengen-agreements, refugee-policies carried out by airline companies, and a groping pollution control the old borders will hardly exist in the long run.

What has up to now been done in the way of reforming jurisprudence on a national scale has had the purpose of pushing the borders and nothingness further towards the horizon. But strictly speaking – as an example – the European Union's judicial establishment-process is continuously based on the geo-centric world conception. The EU rules are valid within this framework, but the consequences they may have outside is not the concern of jurisprudence.

A judicial world conception, or perhaps more than one, which takes its starting point in a world as a coherent whole will undoubtedly have to settle with many doctrines and assumptions.

Which norms unite a world which has no real recognized central authority? Where are such norms created, by whom, and how are they enforced?

In this connection I am not in particular referring to international law, which to a large extent – as the concept implies – is a child of the geo-centric world conception and the national monocentric law-systems. International agreements, and especially those under the UN as they have developed during the last quarter of a century, play, of course, a very significant role in the process towards developing a new worldwide system of justice.

The problem with such an international judicial system has, however, always been the question of law enforcement. No central global authorities have such competence and power that they can enforce international law. For the same reason it has, for a long time, been discussed within judicial theory whether international law in fact could be regarded as law. Whether something was "law" has for a long time been determined by the ability of enforcement by central authorities.

Attempts have been made to establish institutions and authorities endowed with a certain aura of being a central authority. Important examples in this category are the UN-forces and the war-crimes tribunals. They have not, however, had such competence and power that they have been able effectively to secure the observance of only a small part of the many international agreements which are in function.

So far international agreements can only with difficulty be enforced from below as they are generally not created from below. They are not necessarily – maybe even very rarely – the result of a public demand and of the joint and persistent achievements of many interest-groups.

So, only limited and informal means can be found to secure their enforcement.

The question is whether we are now entering an era in which the norms are created by the general public. Is it conceivable and possible to see the development of a "Global Law" which is instituted not by the judicial establishment as has been the case in modern times but maybe rather by ordinary people and the public in general?

Are the many regional and global NGOs and the all encompassing worldwide networks together with the transnational and multinational corporations creating such a global law? Do they in fact define the norms for dealing with disarmament, the trading of women from the Third World to the First World, viable tourism and investments, rationalizations, etc.

I believe that a new global law will be based on horizontal relations rather than on vertical relations between state and citizens which has been the case so far.

Such horizontal, economic, social, ecological relations do not necessarily create equality nor justice. But that is nothing new with regard to the consequences and content of nation law.

Presumably, norms in a global context will not, to the same degree as in the nation state, be created due to dictation or democratic representation. The norms will rather be created through negotiation, persuasion and seduction (mainly through films and advertising) and a certain degree of consideration.

A world in which "global law" will come to play a greater role will not necessarily become a more ideal world. But it will be a world with new and demanding challenges for all those dealing with normative orders, being it professionally, politically, strategically, philosophically or in any other conceivable way.

Otherness in Encounter

Thinking Folk Identity, Democracy and Civil Society with the Help of Martin Buber

Henning Eichberg

"Once when I was a child I read an old Jewish legend which I could not understand. It said nothing but this: "Outside the gates of Rome, a leprous beggar is sitting and waiting. This is the Messiah." At that time I came to an old man and asked him: "What does he wait for?" And the old man answered something which I did not understand at that time and first later on have learned to understand; he said: "For you."

A Difficult Legend

In 1910, when Martin Buber (1878-1965) told this beggar story, the situation was marked by deep national unrest all over Europe. Empires were breaking down – the Ottoman Empire, the Czarist Empire, the Habsburg Empire – national people's revolutions shook several established states, and democratic self-determination seemed to be making its way. The national question was the order of the day, and dependent peoples tried to make themselves the subject of their own history. But from the longer perspective we know that this was the same time that Western colonialism all over the world reached its zenith, finally marked by the Italian conquest of Libya in 1911. The capitalist world market became established, and Western sports served as indicator of neocolonial cultural hegemony. What happened around 1910 was not the start of an era of democracy and peace, but of war and subsequent Fascism.

(Some elements of this description may remind us of the actual era after 1968/89. Indeed, it is not by accident that today we can turn back to compare these historical situations).

At that time of unrest and change, Martin Buber was one of the most outstanding philosophers of (social) identity, a long time before the word itself – folk identity, national identity, cultural identity – was widely used. (This was first introduced by the psychoana lyst Erik H. Erikson in 1950). Buber developed the most extensive theory of folk and folk identity with its centre in the "dialogical principle". On the one hand, folk identity, according to Buber, was not just objectively there. But on the other hand it was more than only a subjective confession. The whole work of Martin Buber moved again and again around this "more" – more than the objective, more than the subjective – trying to define and to describe the third position.

As in the beggar story: The Messiah is not the master of a powerful colonial empire. He is a beggar, sitting in illness and misery outside the gates of the empire. The Jewish folk question is related to this place outside. There is – on the one hand – no pompous objectivity around who "we are" (as Jews or whoever). There is no "It" constituting a sort of national "substance" of identity nor a proof of the greatness of this identity, in terms of political power, technological inventions, results in sports or splendour of arts. But neither – on the other hand – is Jewishness only a question of individual subjective invention. It is more than an invented nationality which easily can be denied by other subjectivities. The Messiah is there, indeed, but he is waiting. The identity of the people – *Volk*, folk – is fundamentally bound to a relation: The Messiah is waiting "for you". The encounter is the point.

The Thou is the third position beyond It and Me, beyond objectivity and subjectivity. It marks a relation, and relationship is in the centre of identity. Thus, the You is not as banal, as problem-free or purely grammatical as it might seem. It constitutes the central point of human existence and by this the point of gravity of the folk question – and of socialism and religion as well. Folk means: It is you, all this is about.

Zionism and Mystics

The philosophy of the You has a biographical depth. Martin Buber was born in Vienna in 1878. His parents divorced soon after his birth, and his mother disappeared from his life when he was three years old. This loss contributed to the experience that the I-you relation would rise as a fundamental problem – a problem which Buber turned into a chance.

Martin Buber grew up with his grandparents in Lemberg. The milieu of his youth was one of prosperous bourgeoisie, of Jewish community and of multicultural folk communication. Around him, people spoke German, Yiddish, Hebrew, Ukrainian and Polish.

From 1896, Buber studied philosophy and history of art in Vienna, later also in Leipzig and Zurich. He became interested in neo-romantic literature, in Nietzsche and in the German mystic tradition – Nicolaus Cusanus, Paracelsus,

Jakob Böhme, Meister Eckhart. At the same time he became active inside the milieu of early Jewish nationalism and participated in the developing discussions of Zionism: Is there anything like a Jewish "folk"?

The years from 1904-1912, however, brought a deep break-through into the life of Martin Buber. For some time he retreated from political Zionism and discovered – probably on the base of his own life crisis and some personal visionary revelations – the world of Hassidic mysticism. While finishing his doctoral dissertation about German mystical thought, he began to retell and edit the Hassidic legends which had their roots in the spiritual movement of Eastern Jewry, starting with Rabbi Israel (called Baal-Schem-Tow) in the eighteenth century. That this rich heritage of Eastern European culture was preserved as a literary reminiscence – while genocide under Hitler and Stalin destroyed its base, the Eastern Jewry – can thankfully be attributed to Martin Buber's work of collection.

The retelling, however, was more than a mere reproduction. It lead to Buber's main work "I and Thou" which was published in 1923.

When Martin Buber afterwards returned to Zionism, this happened on a new base. Now he was able to distinguish clearly between two forms of nationalism. The one nationalism he saw as a signal, as a cry for help from the loneliness of the human being experiencing the societal alienation of modern existence; this nationalism is a striving for togetherness. The other nationalism represented the alienation itself, turning one's own nationality against other peoples in aggression; this nationalism is the hybris in face of otherness.

Buber now tried to relate his own cultural Zionism to the nationalism of the first type: national self-identification being the transcendence of modern time. This included, however, a persisting struggle with the other nationalism which in the case of Zionism meant to expel the Arabs from Palestine and to erect the "purified" Jewish state. In contrast the folk nationalism – which Martin Buber was engaged in – should aim towards a binational Palestine, Jewish and Arab in character at the same time, a dialogical culture between European and Asian spirituality.

This was a hard consequence to draw especially for the assimilated and prosperous Western Jewry. If we really take the greeting "Tomorrow in Jerusalem" seriously, thus was Buber's argument, then this means a Re-Asiaisation – or rather: a new Asiaisation – of Jewish identity. For the Jewish bourgeoisie who looked down with contempt to the Eastern Hassidic kaftan Jew as well as down to the "primitive" Arab, this would sound as no less than a provocation.

Cooperative Socialism and Folk Education

Buber's concept of folk nationalism was, thus, related to a social dimension. More concretely, it had socialist and critical implications, and these were far from being restricted to the Jewish people. Alienation in industrial modernity cannot be abolished by state actions or by the strategy of a political party. But it challenges towards an alternative experiment. Socialism is a permanent effort, not a system. Gustav Landauer, Buber's friend from the Munich bohème, developed the idea of "village socialism". By cooperative association – the anarchist project – human beings can oppose capitalist alienation.

The idea of associative cooperation finally migrated to Palestine and was translated into societal practice, in the form of the kibbuz. The kibbuz united the approaches from Eastern European socialism and the cooperative idea of the German youth movement to which Buber also contributed. Or to say it in its paradoxical logic: While the neo-romantic idea of alternative communities developed by the German youth movement failed in Germany itself, it succeeded at another place – in Palestine. This was brought about by the mediation of Martin Buber who gave the cooperative striving for a socialist community a philosophical base. Life and production in cooperative association means: to say "you" by practice. Socialism is no system and in no way any state system – rather is it the opposite of state. Socialism is the dialogical principle in social action.

The ideas of folk identity and of the associative cooperation met with what became a main contribution of Buber's to Zionist practice: the idea of education.

A people's national action, went Buber's argument, would remain without continuity if one could not transfer its experiences between the generations. But in which institutional form could one build bridges from one generation to the other? Here, Buber hinted towards the Danish poet and educationalist N. F. S. Grundtvig and recommended the Danish *folkehøjskole* (folk academy) to his fellow young Zionists. In the *folkehøjskole*, learning develops by the living word between teachers and students, between old and young, by living together and by dialogical practice. But the living word includes the living silence. Therefore, the word as the centre of the *folkehøjskole* should be supplemented by what had been discovered by the German youth movement: the togetherness of bodily work, of play and dance, of the experience of nature and of bodily movement – the common silence when night is falling at the edge of the wood.

In 1919 Buber himself founded the Free Jewish Academy in Frankfurt/Main, and from this time he consequently tried to build up a Jewish adult education. His main project in this frame became the translation of the Hebrew Bible into German. Martin Buber's tragedy was that this great project of Jewish-German translation was finished at the moment when the German-Jewish people was on the way to become extinguished.

When Nazi anti-semitism grasped power in Germany in 1933, Martin Buber immediately and voluntarily dropped his professorship of religion at the Frankfurt University. In 1935 he was forbidden any public activity, and in 1938 he emigrated to Palestine where he became professor of social philosophy at the Hebrew University of Jerusalem.

From this time, Buber became the most wellknown cultural personality of the new Israel world-wide, but also its most controversial thinker. In part, this controversial aspect was a result of the pro-Arab orientation of his cultural Zionism, but also of aspects of his thinking which – by a certain Jewish orthodoxy – could be seen as being a heretical philosophy. At his funeral in 1965, Arab students laid flowers on his coffin which (or in spite of the fact that it) was covered by the Israeli flag.

But Buber's dialogical understanding of folk identity had no chance at that time in Israel – as elsewhere. It was deeply non-synchronous.

"You Tree"

In his small book "I and Thou", his main philosophical work, Martin Buber expressed what has been called "the Copernican act of the twentieth century": the discovery of the You.

In a poetical form, Buber tried to explicate the question what it means to say "you" to another being. If I say "it" about a tree, the tree will appear as an object of experience and/or as a thing of practical use. There are, indeed, many different nuances possible: I can regard the tree as a picture of forms and colours, I can classify it in a system of biological varieties, I can analyze it under the aspect of natural laws – transformation of energies, evolution, physical statics – , I can measure it by different parametres, I can saw it into useful pieces. But even if I experience the tree by its poetical qualities and describe its smell, sound and flavour in lyrical terms, it will always remain an It, separated from myself. I am no tree.

But I can also say "you" to a tree. This turn, suddenly, changes all for me by radically changing the whole relation. "You tree." By the Thou, a relation becomes existant between me and the other. The tree keeps, it is true, all the elements which had characterized it as an It: colour and chemical substance, smell of resin and rustling of the leaves, biological circulation and value of production, measure and picture. And yet, it becomes something fundamentally other. One new feature is that the tree as "you" appears as a wholeness for me. And another is that – in Buber's words – "relation is reciprocity." It is neither your materiality, nor your "soul" nor the "idea" of a tree which I meet by turning towards "you tree". But it is you yourself – as the other in the configuration of the encounter.

The difference between the It and the Thou does not leave, finally, the I untouched. The I or my Self turning towards the tree as an It, is another one than the I saying you to the tree. The I as such – an essence which is independent of these modes of relation – does not exist. The I is fundamentally determined by the Thou.

This pattern of dialogical encounter is existential. As the example of the relation to the tree shows, the dialogical priciple has an important environmental dimension, too. Buber founded what could be called a philosophy of deep-ecology. But his main interest was directed towards the human and social relations.

Under the aspect of human development, Buber's point is that it is not the I that marks the origin and starting point of life, neither of the individual human being nor of the whole of humanity. This goes confrontationally against the basic assumption of Western ego-centrism which postulates the evolutionary and logical priority of the I before the you, of the individual before society and community. It is not as an I that we start our way, Buber underlines, but as a little child our life begins in a you-world, inside and outside the body of its mother. It is only at a later point of development that the child discovers the objectivity of the surrounding It and the subjectivity of its own Self or I. The You has an important developmental priority.

Seen in a historical perspective one has to state a – tragic – necessity which permanently drives the transformation from Thou to I and It. The process of history and society promotes and accelerates the reification of relations.

"Every Thou in the world is by nature subjected to the destiny to become an It." History is alienation. There is no way back into the womb of the great mother. The appeal "Back to the Thou" would be nothing but a romantic dream, a naive sentimentality.

This does not, however, in any way justify the acceptance of the "dictatorship of the proliferating It" without resistance or critical attention. Buber always kept the perspective of cultural critique and of socialist alternative in mind. The dialogical principle is not only descriptive, it has also ethical contents. For the human being, the I-you relation permanently challenges towards a third way of encounter with the world and with oneself, transcending beyond the relations of I-it and I-I. Therefore: No illusion about the restoration of an ideal and sound you-world. But on the other hand: Never forget what makes up the core of human existence, the relation to the other as "you". The dialogical encounter is possible and – in spite of the expansion of the It – the deepest duty of the human being. The you-relation is the place of love.

The Eternal Thou, the Living Word and the Body

In the last part of his book Buber approaches the theogical point of the Thou. What people call "God" is nothing but a great You, the eternal Thou. How could human beings relate to each other as "you" if the precondition of man's possibility to say "you" was not existing. Prayer and sacrifice are concrete forms of turning towards the eternal Thou by words and actions. This means that God is nothing which can be talked about as an It or He; God can neither be described nor interpreted, nor explained, nor theologically systematized by dogma and catechism – nor only named. God is only what the human being can say "you" to.

Also in this case, however, alienation shows its power as reification. "Belief" and theology make God a being which theologians postulate to know about – an object of knowledge and a monological He. God as the contents of belief and as an object of cult becomes an It. But meditation and mystical experience can open the way towards a dialogical encounter again and again.

All this is more than only some abstract philosophy and more than a trialectical game of terminology. The philosophy of Thou contains – as Buber's life has shown – politics, social and cultural critique and not least a practical pedagogy (or anti-pedagogy).

Dialogical education – seen from Buber's point of view – means, that hearing has priority before reading, learning has priority before knowing. Education means to meet face to face and life to life – body to body, work to work, family to family, song to song. Grundtvig had once called this "the living word" – a word which has not become crystallized in "dead" letter and print but flows dialogically between living human beings so that it is not least the teacher who learns from the student. Teaching is learning – education is reciprocity in free exchange.

The word is the main medium of this encounter, but not the word as a lexical term or grammatical unit – "it" – but as rhythm and intonation, as poetical sound and picture, as a crossing of gesticulation and meaning. The word of dialogical communication is mantra. It is what Buber has called *Sprachleiblichkeit*, a living language-body. And finally the whole of the body is the base of dialogue. As Baal-Schem-Tow expressed it: "To learn to see, that all bodily existence contains holy life and that all can finally be lead back to this root and thus be kept holy".

Democracy is not only One

The you/it approach casts new light upon the question of democracy. Democracy is a complex set of relations and not a simple "thing" which can be treated in the terms of "it".

Some traditions of Western understanding of democracy focus on the written constitution. The constitution is not only regarded as a book of law, which is fundamen tal for administrative practice. But the constitution is made the object of veneration or there is even defined a constitutional "spirit" demanding patriotic "love". This is the case in West German *Verfassungspatriotismus* where the constitution at the same time is made the base for defining enemies, *Verfassungsfeinde*.

Another Western tradition, more down-to-earth, focuses on the rules and regulations of election and representation as the core of democracy. Democracy is regarded as a set of rules how to replace one government by another with some formalized consent of the main part of the population.

In some way the Danish understanding of democracy conflicts with both models. On the one hand, one appreciates the historical Danish constitution, and people engage for the democratic rights which it includes – among others the free right of association and the right not to send one's child to school – but it is not "the spirit of our constitution" which constitutes the base of

Danishness nor is the constitution a mechanism to define enemies of the state. On the other hand, the formal rules of voting and representation are taken seriously in Denmark, too, but they are not regarded as the core of democracy. Democracy is rather seen as a practice of community, of free association and selfdetermination which unfolds between the elections. Democracy is a way of life, as both the Grundtvigian tradition, the socialist tradition and the radical and humanistic theory (Hal Koch 1945) have stated, however differently they have interpreted the contents of democracy.

The main differences between the models of democracy – constitution, rules, way of life – can be understood better with Martin Buber's concepts in mind. Both the constitution and the rules are important, but they are forms of reification, crystallizations of processes which constitute the real base of living democracy. They are "it", while democratic life is based on peoples' ability permanently to enter into dialogical exchange with each other and to say "you" to each other. Democratic quality – in a Danish as well as in a Buberian understanding – is created neither by the perfectness of rules nor by the effectiveness in "defending the constitution against enemies", but by the quality of dialogical relations inside the people as *folk*.

It is here, in the dialogical life dimension of democracy, that its real problems arise. What are the preconditions of turning to each other as "you", in politics? – There are class barriers forbidding I-you relations. There are differences of language blocking the flow of dialogue. That is why there is a certain relation – but not identity – between *demos* and *ethnos*, the democratic people and the cultural folk. But the main problem is a matter of attitude – or of a socio-psychological character. Traumatic experiences, traditions of taboo and the reification of power relations can work against the Thou. That is why folk academies, free associations and cooperative life – as kibbuz socialism – are so important to furnish a real base for the democratic dialogical encounter.

Here Martin Buber delivered a draft of philosophy for what today is called the civil society. The state as the sphere of public order is the field of constitution and election, of representation and administration, all this having strong tendencies towards a reification of rules – and towards power and hierarchies. Legal democracy can unfold here, but the living democratic exchange meets strong barriers in the machine of the state. This is a problem even in the Scandinavian countries where the state is regarded not so much as a structure of power, order, and military but of welfare, balance, and equality. The market as the other sector is the sphere of commercial exchange, of production and consumption. It secures the distribution of goods ("it") and a certain freedom of self-realisation ("I"). These are the conditions of democracy, but no guarantees of democratic life itself. The free democratic exchange is rather at home in the third sector, the civil society with its non-profit social activities. In the world of associations, cooperative work and voluntary action, the social Thou has its central place. Meeting each other in dialogue and I-you relation is the characteristic feature of civil life and civil culture – or what in Danish is called *folkelig* life. Because the concept of civil society describes what other languages and cultural traditions – German, Nordic, Slavic – have understood as *Volk*, *folk* or *narod*.

Global Civil Society?

Consequently, there cannot be expected one global understanding of culture, because there is not only one global language – and language cannot be global because of the deep differences of collective identities and historical experiences – and because of the trialectics of I, It and Thou as well as the tensions between state, market and civil society. But how is the actual globalization related to these patterns and processes?

Global are primarily some dominant tendencies of the market transferring wares all over the world, and that is why commercial activity is the driving force of the actual overall process of globalization. With the goods, screen fictions of life are following – and pidgin American as a new means of communication.

This globalization contrasts with the state which is – and has always been in history – characterized by limits, by certain national or imperial borders. Modern democracy as a public affair has been connected with the public sphere of the nation state, whilst outside the nation state – in multinational empires – the development of democracy has been hampered by ethnic colonial unbalances. But the tension between the globalization of the market and the nationalization of the state is not the whole story.

Civil society constitutes a third pattern also in relation to globalization. It is more connected to the concrete: to the local dimension and to the bodily encounter face to face. In this respect no global folk and no global experience exist. And democracy as a form of civil life is regional, only in certain cases national, and certainly not global. But this is not the whole story, either.

Thinking the globalization problem with the help of Martin Buber's categories means that the most global relation seems to be the relation to the It. While "it" – goods, currencies, sport achievements in centimetres, grams and seconds – can be defined, measured, standardized etc. irrespectively of place, territory and social connection, the subjective I (or We) is always specific and can – in principle – not be communicated in its full content to an understanding from the outside. The thou-relation is specific and concrete, too, but in another way. I can say "you" only to a concrete being, turning to it with my full presence, situationally. Living democracy is here and now by common action of concrete human beings, and living peace is here and now as well. But the possibility to turn towards a You is common to all human beings. It is universal or – in Buber's words – related to an Eternal Thou.

However, concerning the global realization of a dialogical democracy, however, Martin Buber's philosophy gives both encouragement and warning. The alienation going from Thou to It is not only a way of evil intention, it is also related to the limits and limitedness of human bodily existence. If the body is the holy root of human existence, this means that we have to live – voluntarily, with joyful accept – with our limits.

These limits of the human bodily existence become visible and experienced just by the globalization of the networks which are developing beyond the civil societies. The NGOs meet in a conference culture which is characterized by hotel life, screen contact, aircraft traffic, standardized halls of conferences, simultaneous translation systems and pidgin English. The class selection of this neo-colonial world is linked to a reduction of life dimensions: no children, no families, no manual work, very few peasants, few women, no games or dances.

Thus civil societies meet problems which can be compared to those of the state sector when public communication is moving towards a global level. This demands a sceptical and permanently self-critical attention to the concrete bodily dimensions of encounter in the inter-folk networks of civil societies.

The Eternal Thou is there, indeed, but it is not easy to organize people under its premises. Already in the discourse about the Thou, it is tendentiously changing shape towards an It. The Eternal Thou is, as Martin Buber's legend told, not a triumphant emperor, but a beggar at the gates of the large town.

Scepticism and Hope

In this connection it may be helpful to remember the more sceptical version which Franz Kafka gave, few years after Buber, to the story of waiting at the gate. In *Vor dem Gesetz* (1914), Kafka turned the beggar-messiah story of "you" and hope somewhat upside down.

A man from the country side approaches the gate of the Law. However, he does not meet a beggar, but a guard who forbids him to enter. The man waits for permission. He waits and waits – and finally he dies. But while dying, he learns the truth from the guard, "Nobody could enter here but you, because this gate was only made for you. Now I am going to close it."

At this gate, the dialogical You does not unfold. The entrance remains closed. The powerful It dictates – and consequently despair, alienation, and death are following. But in the moment of death, the flow of dialogue and hope arises again – as the memory of a lost chance.

The human existence is placed somewhere between these two stories of Franz Kafka and Martin Buber. Democracy, civil society and peace have their place in-between as well. Between It and You, between death and love. And there is no alternative.

A Philosophy for World Education

Mabud Fatema Kabir

Human beings are social animals and the foundation of their lives and happiness lies with society. It is not possible to live a happy human life without a tangible moral and social philosophy. A true philosophy of life must encompass the ideas of individual freedom in the context of humanity at large – in other words, the global society. To be universal, such a philosophy must accept equal rights of all human beings as its first principle. It must also look forward to a better future for the whole of mankind. The concept of "World Education" fits in very well with such a philosophy.

The essence of education is communication. The human species distinguishes itself from the rest of the animal kingdom by virtue of its communication skills. Deep human feelings can be communicated even without resorting to languages. Spoken languages at first enabled man to communicate with fellow human beings who were present at the same place at the same time. In the course of time, the power of human communication transcended limitations of both space and time. With the communication explosion of our times, the scope and significance of World Education has become even brighter.

The concept of World Education is not a new idea in the region of the world from where I come. Our great poet, Rabindranath Tagore, was a firm believer in humanism and in the philosophy of World Education. He propagated this idea vigorously during the early part of this century. To give this idea an institutional shape, Tagore established a hermitage called the Santi-Niketan (Above of Peace) which was a meeting place of different cultures. In the course of time it has grown into a university. Tagore was a source of inspiration for the generation of his time, including both Mahatma Ghandi and Jawaharial Nehru. Until the Second World War, those were days of great optimism all over the world.

During and soon after the Second World War, there were talks of a new world order. The United Nations was established but soon it became apparent that it was neither powerful enough nor adequate to meet the needs of a global society. By its very name, the UN recognizes divisions and divergences between the nations. The UN is more like a lump of coal, whereas what humanity needs is a diamond. Without a great quantum leap forward, mankind shall never reach the Diamond – that cherished goal of all great thinkers and philosophers.

During the middle of this century, the concept of a Psycho-social evolution was much in vogue. Proponents of this philosophy (e. g. Julian Huxley and Teilhard) spoke of converging forces (mental or spiritual) of humanism leading mankind towards its final unification. It was then a bipolar world and unity seemed near at hand – just from two into one. Such optimism died its premature death in the aftermath of the Cold War. Now the Cold War is over, but still there is no sign of a change of the mind. The hollowness of the idea of a New World Order becomes apparent day by day from squabbles over local wars, trade talks, environment and human rights. In this context, whether psycho-social forces follow politico-economic forces or vice-versa is still a matter of debate.

Communism was not only a political force but also a strong moral force – the only important one of that kind that came out of the Western civilization. It was also not based upon religion or nationalism. The Russian variety of communism was discarded because it led to a repressive society that kept individuals down and disowned. Russia's own long history of despotism may be responsible for this misfortune, not the communist ideology. With the demise of communism, the West has mostly lost its claim on the moral leadership of the world. There is already a sense of cultural decline among western thinkers, and there seems to be a loss of direction in which countries are going.

Somehow the optimism and self-confidence of yesterdays have abruptly melted away. Moral and psychological questions are being raised about the assumptions on which the so called "free societies" of the West are based. The drug culture, increasing crimes, breakdown of the family structure and values, environmental degradation, and a prolonged fear of a nuclear holocaust have had their accumulating affects on the western mind. Meanwhile, a majority of the world's population living in the developing countries are striving for their bare survival under the dual scourge of poverty and overpopulation.

The disparity in wealth between the countries is becoming wider day by day. In 1994, the ratio between the annual per capita GNP of the poorest country (Rwanda with $80) and that of the richest (Switzerland with $37,230) was 1:474 (Sourse: World Development Report 1996; World Bank). Never in the history of mankind has there been such a great disparity in wealth and standard of living between countries. Such great disparities are inconsistent with the concept of a global society or World Education and, in the long run, are not sustainable.

The driving force of the industrial revolution has exhausted itself in the North, but for the world as a whole this revolution is still very incomplete. Only about one third of mankind has fully gone through this revolutionary process; the rest of mankind has yet to do so. For the world as a whole, the emerging spirit of the Industrial Revolution is still very much alive and powerful. The North can overcome its present ideological crisis if it joins its forces with that of the South in a common global struggle for a rapid industrialization of the world. Denmark as the world's leading aid donor to poor countries (in terms of GNP allocation) knows very well that developing countries are more in need of trade, direct investment, and technology transfer than aid from the rich countries.

For World Education to succeed we need first of all a common global social philosophy, acceptable by and large to most of the people in the world. With completely different socio-economic backgrounds in different countries, this may never come. Further, such a philosophy can not be based upon logic alone; it must also derive its strength from spirituality which is the common denominator of humanity and the greatest source of human energy. When I say spirituality, I do not mean religion or ideology. Human spirituality is not confined to religion alone – it is much wider.

Human rights is a catchy cliché but contradictionary even in its definition. How there can be the same human rights everywhere unless there are common shared values and equitable status and privileges? Rights and privileges go together; it is impossible to separate them. So long mankind remains fragmented, "human rights" shall also remain fragmented.

When President Jiang Zemin of China or Prime Minister Mohathir Mohammad of Malaysia point out at the western arrogance of insisting that their conception of human rights is the best and the universal one, it rings a bell in most eastern minds. It should also make a western mind ponder about the negative aspects of their own societies. Also one should not forget that a major part of humanity are still living most degraded lives under the ageless burden of poverty and oppression in a world order that has been imposed and is being perpetuated, mainly by the power and dictum of western countries.

All the poor in the world want to become rich like the people of the rich countries. If the world's political and economic power remain distributed as they are, there is not even the slightest chance of their dreams to be fulfilled. With growing population the poor are becoming poorer every day. Further, global resources and the environment would never sustain such a situation. Is there a doomsday looming ahead for mankind in the twenty-first century? Logically speaking, the answer is probably "yes". However, for optimists there is still a ray of hope. As past history shows, human beings have not always been logical when faced with serious problems of survival.

The process of globalization has already started, but its outcome is still uncertain. It is still mostly driven by national and commercial forces without consideration of common human aspirations or goals. The question is, what we can do individually and collectively to make the process more humane, compassionate and oriented towards predetermined goals. Ordinary individuals like most of us can do very little, working on our own in isolation. However, when many individuals join their hands together to form a global association for a common purpose, they can become a powerful force, and sometimes achieve miracles. The Philosophy for World Education should lead one to such an association.

World Education is only the means – not the end. Before launching a worldwide association, one must clearly understand to what ends it is directed, and whether such ends are achievable. The cat in the book Alice in Wonderland said, "If you don't know where you are going, the road will take you there." This is only another way of saying that if we do not know where we are going, we shall not reach anywhere. In spite of what all the wise men of the world through ages have been saying and pointing at, the shortsighted humankind has only been moving in circles.

Those who support the Philosophy of World Education have to come to a broad consensus among themselves about the distant goals for which they would like to work together and pool their resources. Such goals, even if they are hypothetical, should be achievable, and spelled out clearly and unambiguously and not cloaked in dogmatic terminology or mystic allegory. Creating yet another sect (like the Bahais or the Scientologists) will not bring mankind together. What is needed is a philosophy and agenda to support a broad "unity among utmost diversities". Once the goals are set, it is possible to outline and adopt a global project to achieve those goals.

The goals for Global Education should not be adopted arbitrarily by any elitist group sitting at the top in a global conference; those should evolve through a "bottom-up process" with the participation of many diverse kinds of individuals and groups spread all over the world. One possible way is to use the global communication highway, namely the Internet. World Education should set up a Home Page in the Web with linked regional, sub-regional, and local nodal points. While inviting and allowing local chapters, national identities should be generally avoided. However, it has to be seen that diverse ethnic, racial, and minority groups are included in the network. In whatever association, national or international, the test of democracy is not in ensuring the rights, privileges, and representations of the majority, but in ensuring those of the minorities. This could be a dictum for the philosophy of world education.

The first task for the networking groups would be to develop a set of hypothetical goals for mankind, to be achievable, say be the year 2100 A. D. There will be many divergent views and ideas, and these have to be filtered for reaching a consensus on common goals. This can be done first at the regional or sub-regional level. Once a set of goals are identified, the logical frame for a project can be built up in a reverse sequence as follows: Goals $\Leftarrow$ Purpose $\Leftarrow$ Targets $\Leftarrow$ Outputs $\Leftarrow$ Activities. Thus activities would be identified with measurable outputs and indicators which are expected to lead to specified outcome as Targets; these targets are expected to achieve certain identified purposes leading ultimately to the achievement of the set goals. What is described above, is a standard Log Frame for developing a purposeful goal-oriented project.

Such a project would be ambitious and its success would depend on many assumptions at various stages of its implementations. The important thing is to identify the critical assumptions, so that contingencies or alternate pathways can be thought out beforehand in case of failed assumptions. Since purposes and goals in the case of World Education are rather distant, measurable proxy indicators instead of real indicators may have to be chosen. To a great extent the choises of activities would depend on available resources. One prime activity could be the use of a satellite TV channel for the dissemination of ideas. There is no harm in using global commercial advertisements for sustaining such an effort, provided the overall purpose of World Education is not compromised or undermined. After all, the transnational corporations are already playing a leading and vital role in the globalization process. However, all transnational corporations are not really global. A transnational corporation is truly global when its total capital investment in any one country is less than half of its total investment all over the world. World Education could very well promote such global corporations.

Side by side with the development of a global communication network, World Education also needs gradually to develop a worlwide organizational network. Here again, the local chapters should not be nation based – they should be local, regional, or subregional without national identification. The membership of each chapter should be open to all men and women, irrespective of their nationalities, race, sex, religion, or ethnicity. Deliberate efforts will have to be made by each chapter to maintain within itself an equity in respect of nationalities, sex, race, and ethnicities. The setting up of a global communication network of World Education is probably more important and urgent than setting up its local and regional chapters.

For the last few hundred years, mankind has been entrenched on the back of a many headed monster – still acclaimed, glorified, and anointed all over the world as "nationalism". This monster may get finally slain to be buried once and for all time to come through World Education. Let us hope that day is nor far away.

What is the Link Between Education for Life and World Education?

Edicio dela Torre

When I was asked by the Association for World Education to speak on this topic I initially thought it would be an easy taks. However, the more I thought about it the more I started feeling nervous, which is not my usual self. I wondered why. When I teach public speaking at our folk school in the Philippines we identify four main reasons for getting nervous: a) we have little experience in public speaking, b) we know little about the topic, c) we do not know the audience, or d) we have a low esteem of ourselves.

None of the reasons seem to apply. Anyway, in case of doubt, I advise the students to talk about their personal life experience since that is the topic they know better than anyone else. So I will follow my advice and discuss our theme according to my life experience of it.

A Four-Quadrant Framework:
Local, National, Inter-National, Global

But first, a framework that I find useful. Last month I was at a meeting in Thailand, and a Korean friend proposed a four-quadrant framework which I like: Local, national, inter-national, global.

Local links to national, but also to global without passing through the national. What I found especially useful in distinction between global and international. Global is world and is not merely an aggregate to the 184 or so member national-states of the UN. Perhaps ecumenical and ecological would be the closest concept. Ecumenical refers more to people and culture, while ecological emphasizes the integration of nature. Both have their roots in *okios* (household) which is our primary experience of community.

Looking back at my life in the Philippines I realize that one difference between living in the North and the South is that you in the North, especially in Denmark, almost take for granted that you can influence your government (considered the main actor in international relations although this is now under question). You also feel some responsibility for the rest of the world and some capacity for acting beyond borders. This was especially true in the 70s for those who accepted the framework of dependence and underdevelopment.

However, in a country like the Philippines with 65 million people living in 300,000 square kilometres divided into many islands (over 7000 although most people are in 20 islands), the government is quite remote from the ordinary people. It is difficult to think national, much less international.

One scholar hypothesizes that the participants in national discourse are only those who read the English-language national dailies and that is fewer than a million in our country.

A recent encyclopedia of the Cultural Center of the Philippines identifies 51 distinct ethno-linguistic groups in the Philippines. I am a Tagalog which is one of the dominant groups. But I grew up in an island south of Manila and did not have a sense of being national. My consciousness was bound first by my village called barangay San Antonio (all in all there are 42,000 barangays), then at my town called Naujan (there are 1500 towns), and finally my island-province called Mindoro (there are 75 provinces).

The Step from Local to Global

Moving from my local village to study at the town center, my local consciousness linked first to the global before the national. How? Through religion and the Roman Catholic church. Mindoro was considered mission territory, not having its native clergy, and we had missionaries from a religious order founded by Germans across the border in Holland because of Bismarck's "Kulturkampf". They were an international order, so we had Americans and Hungarians in addition to Germans. I started looking at myself as belonging to this international, or is it more accurate to say global community of catholics.

This is true of so-called world religions, especially Christianity and Islam, which consider their baptized believers part of a community that transcends borders. On the other hand, we are also animists and that is another way of local linking with global since animist religions, although very local and contextual, do exhibit common features.

The other link from local to global was through formal education especially since our educational system has been criticized of being quite colonial. I remember reading not just about America, the mythical paradise in our colonial consciousness, but even about Nordic myths, remembering mainly Thor and his hammer. My vocabulary and imagination did expand but without any accompanying experience, the link remained tenuous and peripheral.

The Step from Local to National

I travelled to Manila for my seminary studies, and that was the first in a series of steps that linked my consciousness of local and national. The key link was social issues. As a seminary student, I got involved in land reform issues and the education and organization of peasants. I realized the need for national legislation and government implementation of laws, and discovered the discourse of democratic governance. I also learned to look at our history through these eyes not only of the elite but of the peasants who periodically rose in rebellion, pithily and aptly summed up in a rebel leader's comment,"No uprising ever fails. Each one is a step in the right direction".

Like many social activities which had their awakening in the late 60s my consciousness about global (maybe more accurately international) was forged through the discours on dependence and underdevelopment, and in denouncing US imperialism. Our problem was not just our landlords and a corrupt elite, but the multinationals, and unfair trade and investment relations. Debt was not yet an issue; in fact some national economists were advocating foreign loans as less exploitative than foreign investments.

Our social and political awakening was accompanied by a cultural awakening – a realization of our colonial mentality and the need to strengthen a sense of self-worth and self-reliance. This was couched in the language of national as anti-colonial, or more positively, using Benedict Anderson's happy phrase, as imagined community, both limited and sovereign.

The link between global and national was more marked in so-called development aggression projects when indigenous communities were threatened with inundation and loss of ancestral lands through big dam projects of central government, financed by the World Bank.

Ironically, both my national and global consciousness were further crystallized when I was confined to a very small local place in prison during the Marcos dictatorship. The solidarity letters and visitors from all over the world introduced med to the world human rights community. My future wife who visited me in prison also introduced me to women's rights and global sisterhood. More recently the structural issue of migrant labor and the broader issue of migration further shapes my sense of the links between local, national and global.

How Do We Develop a Sense of Empowerment Together with Enlightenment?

There is more to tell, but given time limits, let me address the theme: Education for life and world education.

At first glance it would seem like an obvious connection. If life is lived at many levels – local, national and global, the education for life (and I may add education From Life) needs to address all these dimensions. But the actual process of awakening and realizing is more complex. I realize that in the Danish tradition educationg for life is linked with enlightenment, "oplysning". Drawing from my Philippine experience I think we *need to have both enlightenment and empowerment.* Empowerment includes awareness, but also a sense of capacity to act effectively.

Because of our many limitations (structurally and even educational methodology) the link betweem education for life and world education is not strong in the South. I would hypothesize that the key link to world education is an awareness being disadvantaged through our relations outside our national borders, and defensiveness, even resentment. The other side of this legitimate feeling is a tendency to think our responsibility is restricted to our borders. Let the powerful worry about the world, and we can blame them for making a mess of it.

It was in fact during my first visit to Denmark, in 1987, that I realized this limitation. I was asked to speak at a workshop on international solidarity and as usual, after presenting the situation in the Philippines one of the questions was, "What can we do to help, in the spirit of solidarity?" I heard the same question wherever I spoke. Of course, concerned citizens in the North can help, and the best of them do so in the spirit of solidarity and a sense of justice. But sometimes, they also talk in hopeful terms about our struggles and wonder why there is no similar mass struggles in the North.

I thought of two points. One, if our analysis accept that poverty in the South and affluence in the North are connected we would logically conclude that struggle in the South and the North are connected: But why do we tend to accept only responsibility for problems in the South? Putting it rhetorically, why share only our pain, and not our hope? For our part, I worry that in the South we tend to think that we have enough problems to worry about within our national borders, unlike those in the North who accept that in addition to acting about their national issue they should also be concerned about issues in other countries, especially former colonies. There is a danger of a subtle sense of moral superiority as if there is moral surplus in the North and moral shortage in the South, at least on international and global issues.

But how does someone from the South care about other countries, including those in the North? How do we forge organic, logical and emotional connections? How do we develop not just learned helplessness, but a sense of empowerment together with enlightenment?

"The Commodification of Desire"

In some way, those questions were still marked by the framework of the 70s with inter-national relations dominant. But the ecological issues of the 80s and the communications-finance issues of the 90s pose them in more complex and urgent terms.

A recent book co-authored by Susan George presents an interesting link between my early local to global links and the most dominant contemporary local to global links. The title is Faith and Credit, and is about the World Bank. She argues that the dominant development philosophy and direction is repeatedly proven wrong in its effects, especially on local communities, but it is still held on to because, like bad religion, it is based on an unquestioning belief that conveniently excludes or explains away any evidence to the contrary. Instead of a mystifying theological language we have an even more mystifying economic language. But the impact, like that of bad religion, is the same on our lives, perhaps even more deadly.

When we discuss economics in our folk high school, we realize how remote the realm of trade and finance is from our consciousness, especially when they go beyond our imaginable local and national circuits. And our sense of disempowerment deepens. I read somewhere that daily around 1 trillion US dollars is traded in the global casino by 22,000 money traders, and that only 12% of this money has a direct bearing on the value and movement of goods and services. Governments and central banks, even in the North, are realizing their diminishing power.

But it is not only the global money. It is also the global communications and what they communicate. In 1974, in prison, I read a pioneering book called *Global Reach* which argued that the terms multinational and transnational were already inadequate to describe the biggest corporations' consciousness and operations. Instead they should be called global corporations. Twenty years later, in 1994, a follow-up book is interestingly titled *Global Dreams*. It argues that the deeper power of the global corporations in their ability to shape our inmost sense of what we want and what it takes to be fulfilled as human beings. I am reminded of another scholar's happy phrase "the commodification of desire". Or more biblically, "Do not be afraid of those who only kill the body. Fear those who kill the spirit and the body".

We can address globalization from the point of view of national communities, represented by the nation-state. This is legitimate. But the specific challenge of AWE and its specific charism is to address globalization from the point of view of the local communities.

Compared to the 70s, there are more favorable material cultural and political conditions for appreciating the local-global connection. Part of the reason is the sense of frustration at the ability of central governments to represent the diversity of local communities and bargain with global forces. Part of the reason is a welcome relization that the local community especially if understood wholistically (in the concept of bio-districts and bio-regions) in where the synergy of life may be forged, in resistance, empowerment and solidarity. To be precise, we are really talking of two processes: local to local and local to global.

The Living Systems are Those That are Selforganizing and Selfrenewing

Tha national-state and national identities are less than half a century old. There are fewer than 200 nations, but there are supposed to be around 5,000 languages and I guess even more dialects. It is not a matter of inventing a universal language like Esperanto, but of realizing the diversity of language and life and underneath them a unity, if only because we share one planet the Earth. There is of course the Gaia hypothesis that looks at the whole earth as a living organism, self-organizing, self-sustaining and self-healing. There may be some insight into this in our Tagalog language where "pakikipagkapwa" or relatedness is one of the keywords, as in Indian "Bless all my relations".

What do these mean for an association like AWE? I think we should be part of those groups and communities who recognize the diversity of life and identities, and yet link these to the whole and emphasize our interconnectedness and shared fate (shared risks and shared hopes). This intersects with inter-national understanding, whether in the realm of peace (avoiding war and arms rate) or in justice and development, in international trade, investment and loans. The recent world summit reminds us of this quite forcefully.

But it is the realm of the spirit, above all, we need to connect, because it is the one resource that is in equal supply all over the world, and it is the key to our renewal. We must contribute to the realization that this is more important and that it is when we connect that we develop not only greater awareness but also power which one writer defines as "our capacity to translate our intentions to action and to sustain it".

I would like to end here, even though dissatisfied with the vagueness of my suggestion. But perhaps we can take comfort from insights of lifesystems theory that the best systems, living systems, are those that are selforganizing and self-renewing. That is the challenge to AWE and that is the way forward. I am happy to join you in this life journey.

Adult Learning Between Global Economy and National Democracy

Ove Korsgaard

ADULT EDUCATION AND TRAINING

What is the role of adult education and training within a context of globalisation? How is adult education effected by the process of globalisation?

In many countries, from Japan to Sweden, the same conclusion is to be heard: If we are to compete, to develop, to survive, the most critical resource to rely on is people's talent and energies. All nations are faced with the fact that knowledge seems to be a still more decisive factor in the industriel production and the global competition.

A great number of national and international reports point to education and training as a key factor in the global economic competition.

The White Book from the European Commission on *Growth, Competition and Employment. Challenges and Ways into the 21st Century* (1993) stresses the importance of a massive effort in the field of education and training. It is pointed out that the competition especially demands the fundamental ability to acquire new knowledge and new skills, e. g. "to learn to learn all through life". The fundamental qualifications today comprise: "The ability to develop one self and function in a complex environment with a high degree of technology".

Another White Book from the European Commission on *Teaching and Learning. Towards the Knowledge-Based Society* (1995) makes it clear, "The countries of Europe today have no other option. If they are to hold their own and continue to be a referencepoint in the world they have to build on the progress made along the road to the Europena Union by more substantial investment in their knogledge base".

Agenda 2000 from the Swedish Ministry of Education (1994) also places importance on highly developed human capital as a key factor in a greater international competition. "Knowledge and competences are the most important prerequisites for successful change. Knowledge will be the most important means to promote Sweden's competitiveness. The culture of learning must characterise our society".

Also in Japan education and training are placed on top of the political agenda. According to professor Yoshio Katagiri education is today the most concerned matter for parents and children in Japan. They live in a so-called "education-record society" where the "war of entrance exam" governs their life[1]. In Japan about 50 pct. of the adult population take part in adult education and training.

Education and training has increasingly become the principal forces for each individual, enterprise, and nation, because:

– education is a decisive factor for income and employment possibilities throughout life,

– education is a key variable for the competitiveness for enterprises on the global market,

– education is of overwhelming importance in determining each nation's position in the global competition.

The concept of education and training throughout life has emerged as one of the keys to the twenty-first century. Education which hitherto has been connected with a certain phase in life has now become a life-long necessity. This implies that a whole lifespan which so far has not been given priority in educational policies has now become the corner-stone of the renewal process of society. Now adult education is part of continuing education and life long learning. Worldwide the participation in adult education and training is highly differentiated on class, gender, race, and ethnic lines as there is a correlation between the levels of prior educational attainment and participation in adult education and training. Unless adult education and training consciously counters the trend it could be contributing to creating an even greater differentiation in society.

Historically, there are two different and important theoretical and ideological stands which argue for life-long learning. The concept was introduced by UNESCO in the late 1960s and it was related to a humanistic: tradition and connected with democracy and selv-development. Around 1980, however, the position of UNESCO was clearly weakened and OECD obtained an increasing influence on the educational policies, specially in Western countries. The new understanding of lifelong learning was based on a neo liberal concept regarding education as an investment in "human capital" and "human resource development". The theory of human capital expressed a view concerning the economic reasons for adult education and training, but had almost nothing to say about democracy and social justice. The humanistic and democratic tradition was more or less replaced by a version framed within a new politic-economic imperative.

In the 1960s the pressure for an expansion of educational opportunities had strong social roots. A more even distribution of investment in education would equalise individual earnings. This assumption was important because it linked the economic justification for an education form with the social demands for equal opportunity. Greater equity in the educational opportunity was seen as a major levelling force in society. It was democratisation through education. Looking at policy documents from various countries, written since the 1980s, the erosion of a commitment to equality and the total dominance of the economic imperative is very evident.

Another significant shift between the 1960s and the 1990s is the use of the terms adult education and training. In the 1960s they coexisted as two separate tracks barely communicating with one another. The former was concerned mainly with democratic, political and cultural issues, whilst the latter was focused on work related skill training. But in the 1990s, at least in some parts of the world, adult education and vocational training are not any longer seen as discrete entities. This move to integration is in UNESCO espressed in using the term "adult learning".

The current discussion about education accentuates highly developed human capital, science and technology to support economic restructuring and greater international competitiveness through increased productivity. The fact that adult education and training is increasingly governed by economic goals makes it necessary to consider the traditional link between adult education, citizenship, democracy, and civil society. There is every reason to place renewed emphasis on the political and moral dimension of education. Globalisation calls for new forms of cooperation, democracy and global governance; although generally acknowledged, in a world of competitiveness among distinct nation states they are as yet only weakly developed. But as described by the Lisbon Group, the logic of globalisation ipso facto demands, in the long term, certain limitations of the mechanisms of competition as a unique principle for modern societies[2]. According to such views, adult education should not only have competition, but also cooperation as a goal. Lifelong education and education for life are not necessarily the same.

EDUCATION FOR DEMOCRATIC CITIZENSHIP

Globalisation forces us to rethink what we take for granted. It is necessary to review some issues in the relation between capitalism, nation-state, democracy and citizenship.

The emergence of a modern understanding of citizenship in the West was associated particularly with the advent of capitalism and of centralised nation states in the sixteenth to the seventeenth centuries. Citizenship was finally given voice as a massively influential political concept in the seventeenth and eighteenth centuries by the world historical events of the English, American, and French Revolutions. The "natural rights" and "Rights of Man" announced by these revolutions, their concepts of "liberty, equality and fraternity" and their attempts to found the modern nation state constitutionally on the will of the people helped construct the modern Western conception of citizenship.

In his classical study *Citizens and Social Class* (1963) T. H. Marshall outlined three phases in the development of citizenship from the sixteenth to the twentieth century: first civil rights, then political rights and then social rights.[3]

The dominant paradigm of citizenship was developed in the postwar West through various forms of "national functionalism". This concept refers to the functional interdependence or symbiosis which was developed and maintained between the major societal sectors namely the economy, policy, and culture and their systems of institutions in modern society. Another way of referring to this type of societal arrangement is to see it as a de facto "national social contract". The contract was formed between democratic nation states and the nationally based and organised industrial capitalist economies to which they played host.[4]

Both the welfare state and the welfare market were central to this accommodation. Capitalism would undertake to deliver employment and income, in return for various state services. The state would undertake to produce and reproduce a relevantly skilled and healthy labour force via an educational and welfare state.

Marshall acknowledged the underlying tension or "war" between capitalism on the one hand and democratic citizenship and social justice on the other. Nonetheless, he also implied that the accommodation between capitalism and democracy in the postwar period represented an event of historical and lasting significance for modern Western society. The "war" could be controlled, the warriors pacified and capitalism "civilised".

However, evidently the "war" is not over. The globalisation of economies makes it more difficult to sustain regulation models which are based on the welfare state and Keynesian policies which have underpinned economic policies since World War II, specially in Western Europe. Keynesianism was premised on the idea that national economies were real. The acceleration in globalisation since the mid 1970s has nevertheless caused a loss of effectiveness of national policies in the sphere of welfare.

Given the failures of the welfare state, arguably a new social contract is needed between capitalism and its host societies.

Looking to the future, it is reasonable to assume that a large part of the future politics of social citizenship will be concerned with an attempt to repair these arrangements at the national state level. In addition new sorts of functional and social contract arrangements at local, regional and global levels are likely to be sought for and to be developed. Citizenship is an important concept in the late twentieth century. Whether in the form of democratic movements, or of nationalist movement, the world historical changes set in motion since the late 1980s in Eastern Europe, Latin America and South Africa have been produced largely by movements of citizens striving to realise or to redefine their citizenship rights and citizen community. In Western Europe the increasing economic, legal and political integration of the European Community is beginning to challenge national sovereignty and citizenship. In addition, it is also beginning to involve the creation of a new transnational European level and sphere of citizen's rights, institutions and community. In North America the meaning of US citizenship is being challenged in many states, not least in California, by the massive growth of the Spanish speaking population. Elsewhere in North America Quebec separatism continues to challenge Canadian nationhood and citizenship.[5]

Feminism involves claims for women's rights and social justice and many of these claims are indeed claims against the state, for instance claims for the satisfaction of basic welfare needs. But many are also claims for equality within the state, the market and civil society, claims for equal citizenship in all arena and at all levels. However, the primary thrust for equity and social justice for women cannot be separated from other inequities based on race, ethnicity, class or geography. They are all interconnected.[6]

Feminism in modern society challenges the masculine structures of the state, the market and civil society; they challenge men in modern society to recognise the existence of a patriarchal order and of the manifold ways in which they both dominate women's lives and benefit from doing so. Advancing the cause of women's equality challenges men to accept a duty to change themselves and to change their ways of relating to women in order to honour those rights. In effect feminism challenges men to accept a duty to act against the patriarchal order in which women are second class citizens and to act for equality, a society of equal citizenship.

Also the ecological movements are concerned with the politics and morality of duty. Of course it champions rights, and it does so in two distinct registers at that. In the first register ecology champions the rights of non humans (animals, the environment, nature etc.). Nature's rights thus imply duties for humans. Ecology thus addresses itself to the often agonising debates and struggles within and between modern states and societies, and indeed within each individual, between on the one hand human needs, desires, and rights and on the other hand duties we impose on ourselves by our recognition, such as it is, of the rights of the non-human.

In its second register ecology champions nature and the environment on behalf of posterity. Thus generations of humans as yet unborn are assumed to have the rights to an environment at least as resource-rich and as undegraded and undamaged as the one the present generation inherited. The "rights of future generations" are thus deemed to impose duties of environmental "stewardship" on all individuals, communities, organisations, and nations.

Like nature, future generations cannot reciprocate the performance of duties. It seems reasonable to argue that in this way an intergenerational moral relationship or community exist in human affairs. This implies that all explicitly or implicitly purely intra-generational conceptions of social justice of the proper distribution of ecological and other forms of welfare must incorporate an inter-generational element which imposes a set of unreciprocated duties on the present generation to provide ecological welfare for future generations.

Ecology challenges the dominant paradigm of citizenship. It expands the sphere of our relevant civil society and citizenship in two ways: it expands this sphere beyond the national state level to the global level and to other ecologically relevant levels from the global to the local; also it expands it beyond the present generation and requires us to consider the inter-generational dimension of our sociality and our moral and citizenship duties.[7]

In the early twenty first century the politics of citizenship will need to go beyond the nation state and the welfare state. They will need to grasp the emerging structural complexity and the new post industrial and post national dynamics influencing citizenship, from family and local levels to the transnational level and the inter-generational sphere. They will need to transform the gendered nature of citizenship to ensure that women become full and equal participants at all levels in all spheres.

The new agendas for politics regarding citizenship in the future must, of course, continue to be concerned with nationally defined citizenship and with the future of the welfare state. But they also need to be sensitive to these new developments.

The period in which it was possible to conceive citizenship in general and social citizenship in national and welfare state terms has clearly come to an end. New positive myths and ideals of citizenship rights are developing, such as those involving notions of "the Earth's rights", the "rights of the unborn" and "global citizenship". They enrich and complicate the more conventional modern myths and ideals relating to citizenship, such as those involving notions of human equality, of place and territorial identity, of nation and heritage.

These new ideals of citizenship opens up possibilities for slowly dissolving the historical connection between nation state and "civil citizen". Such a development would nourish the concept that it is not only national solidarity which counts, but also the global entity.

ADULT LEARNING AND DEMOCRACY

The concept of the nation and of democracy has been considered as cornerstones in modern societies. Historically, the modern type of democracy was born within the frame of a nation state. The national struggles for freedom in the 19th and 20th century were fought in the belief that democracy, human rights and social justice are central elements in the establishment of a sovereign state.

Traditionally, adult education and popular education has played an important role in many democratic movements, connected more with social, political, cultural and personal development than economic development. In the 1970s and 1980s adult and popular education played a crucial role in the national and democratic movements within different countries like the Philippines, Chile, Hungary, Poland and SouthAfrica.

From the begining there was in UNESCO a close connection between adult education and popular education. In the very first article of the Constitution establishing UNESCO, paragraph 2(b), a direct reference was made to popular education, asking the new UN organisation and the member states to "give fresh impulse to popular education and to the spread of culture".[8]

Democracy and the possibility to learn, individually and collectively, have been seen as closely interrelated. It has been a fundamental idea that democracy in the very last instance is built on adult and popular education.

In the liberal tradition adult education is primarily concerned with individual self-empoverment. The goal is to empower the individual's character, abilities and capacities with a sense of unique personal meaning. Adult education means bringing out the individual nature in each man and woman to its true fullness, thus bringing about the expression of their individual uniqueness. Education involves personal transformation and change. In this, education reveals itself to be a human endeavour in which education and change are dynamically dependent, for without education there can be no change and without change there can be no education. In the educational encounter between the individual and other persons, knowledge and understanding are passed on in such a way that they develop a life of their own in the unique experience of the individual person while at the same time bringing about a transformation of how the individual sees the world, and hence feels about it.

In the communitarian tradition adult education is seen as an attempt to empower the "community", the "people", the "folk", or the "class". Adult education has to create a strong sense of utility and initiate a process of nation building. Both the workers' educational movements in different countries and the Folk High School movements in the Scandinavian countries were based on a strong communitarian ideology. The former emphasised the working class as the community, the latter the nation and the "folk". Because democracy has to be built within a community, adult and popular education should not only strengthen the individual as a human being, but also individuals as "political animals". For the last 200 years the nation state has been seen as a necessary community for democracy.

Today, we are witnessing two powerful processes: one towards market economy and the other towards democracy. But the nation state is not the solid frame it was before. New democracies are being built within nations at a time when the nation state is becoming less important because global economic forces are inclined to minimise national borders. South Africa for example needs to unite politically and recognise differences amongst its diverse population of 40 million people who speak eleven language, who have been systematically organised along racial lines, and who vary widely across the division of culture, gender, social class and religion.[9]

The changing relationship between economy, democracy, and adult education also create new problems in old democratic nations. According to professor M. Welton, Canada is in the midst of convulsive changes which has brought the liberal democracy, the liberal tradition for democracy, and the liberal tradition for adult education in a deep crisis: "The two crises – of liberal democracy and of adult education – are inextricably linked". Canadian adult education has traditionally been concerned with issues of social action and public responsibility, and for much of the 20th century contained "moral alternatives to the market". But this tradition has been weakened.[10]

What is the future of this tradition in the age of globalisation? Is it still important to differentiate between education for economic development and education for democratic development?

According to the Nobel prize winner for Peace 1991, Aung San Suu Kyi, Burma, democracy is essential if sustained human development is to be achieved. "The true development of human beings involves much more than mere economic growth. At its heart there must be a sense of empowerment and inner fulfilment"[11] It has to be an important aim of adult learning to support such a sense.

ADULT LEARNING AND CIVIL SOCIETY

The process of democratisation is much more than democratic election. Democracy also represents a value system where each person has equal rights and where those who rule follow a generally accepted code of behaviour. It involves a respect for and adherence to the rules of the game in the sense that not just a top down approach and mentality is prevailing, but also that there is room for a bottom up approach, i. e. that the ordinary man in the local society can influence the agenda, can dismiss the rulers and keep them responsible and accountable.

Democracy is not only a legal system, but a way of life. In other words: democracy depends on a living civil society. The conception of a civil society as a separate area in relation to the market and the state is as old as modern society, but the understanding of what is meant by civil society has changed through history.

The modern understanding af the concept came from the commoners' fight against nobility and absolute monarchy. The civil society became a category of liberty. For liberals the state should only regulate the competition among individuals for their private goods. The liberal conception of the state forbids the state from having a public notion of the good or from using its power to impose some concept of the good on its citizens[12].

It was not possible for all to accept the liberal model, which was built on an alliance between the market and the civil society against the absolute power of the state. From the beginning of modern democracy there was also a communitarian model, based upon the idea that a democratic society can only rest on publicly practised citizens' virtues. In the very last end the prerequisite for both the market and the state is non economic ties of confidence and solidarity. In other words, democracy depends on moral virtues. To build a society is an art which does not originate from the state or from the market, but from the citizenship of the civil society. The key institutions of society, especially the educational system, have to support this art; if they don't democracy will be destroyed.

Neither the working class could accept the liberal model of the civil society. This class regarded the market as a destructive force, therefore, it was not first of all the state but the market which should be tamed.

Within Socialism, this perspective led to two different standpoints. One standpoint was expressed in the conception that the civil society was a bourgeois phenomenon which should be given up. There were only two sectors in society: the market and the state. According to this model, Socialism and the state are two sides of the same coin, namely state-socialism.

The second standpoint was that the civil society, also for Socialism, was an important concept. First and foremost, it is Antonio Gramsci who has pointed out the importance of keeping the civil society as an independent category in the Socialistic thinking. But this three-pole-model had great difficulties within Socialism, standing up against the two-pole model. It was not only in the Communist ideology and practice that civil society went out of sight. Also in

Social Democratic welfare states it was difficult to attach an ideological and practical meaning to civil society. For many years, therefore, civil society was out of the theoretical limelight.

But in the 1980s, the concept had a revival. Impulses for this came foremost from critical intellectuals in Eastern Europe and South Africa. In the concept they found a positive frame for a self-definition in opposition to the totalitarian state systems. Vis a vis the all-encompassing state, the dissidents tried to create a free space where they could live as citizens outside the shadow of the totalitarian state.

Also in different kinds of communitarian thinking, civil society became an important concept in the 1980s. For the communitarians, civil society becomes the place where the individual and society are mutually committed in a morally obligated community[13].

Today, it is widely accepted that the quality of democratic governance depends on the working together of two sides: on one side there is the nature of state institutions and the responsiveness and accountability of state officials; on the other there is the nature of civil society and its ability to exert control over the state apparatus. To do that depends very much on a dynamic and vigorous public sphere.

The public sphere is a central element of civil society. The distinction and the relationship between public and privat spheres have been problematised by feminists in important ways. It is through institutions both in the "public" and "private" domains that members of civil society can engage in informed public debate and action upon matters of common concern, including the way in which power is distributed and developed within society[14].

There are wide variation in the ways people relate to the public sphere that are shaped by their cultural, gendered, raced, classed locations in societies. In some societies only certain categories of citizens are entitled to such participation. But meaningful democracy presupposes the ability of all people to pool their limited resources, to form and develop ideas and programs, put them on the political agenda, and act to support them.

Democracy depends on the favourable organisation of civil society. For it is in the learning life of associations, organisations, movements and study circles that common problems, which reverberate first in individual life histories, are distilled and transmitted in an amplified form to the public sphere.

Up to now the public sphere and civil society have been based on the "international culture of the nation states": the public sphere and the civil society have been seen as phenomena connected to a nation state. In view of globalisation, the public sphere and civil society have to globalise, too, and have to find new channels and fora for communication and cooperation[15].

Increasing globalisation is clearly a two-edged sword. On the one hand, it is quite obvious that it removes competence from the national context, and that globalisation in this way undermines the institutions which hitherto have been used for communication, cooperation and social integration.

On the other hand globalisation, perhaps, opens up new possibilities for a democratic influence on essential common issues which in their nature are about the framework of the nation state. Employment questions, for example, are no longer domestic problems. They have to be dealt with internationally and related to enviromental issues and gender relations. Attempts to democratise are therefore forced to work for the establishment af global democratic structures, including international organs for civil society.

The quite decisive question is, of course, whether democracy can develop outside the shell in which is was born, namely the nation state. According to the pessimists, the relationship between democracy and the nation-state is so close that a democratisation of international structures and institutions is bound to fail. According to the optimists a new understanding of democracy and sovereignty is in the making.

But one thing is sure: if democracy is to transcend the frame of the nation state, there must be a development of a global public sphere and a global civil society. It demands international civil structures and corresponding public experience facilities.

Such structures are hardly present in the international political process. It is first and foremost on the economical and technological level that global integration has taken place. But it cannot be in the interest of civil society to leave the regulation of this integration to market forces alone or to the naked competition between states. Instead, the fight must concern itself with the establishment of as comprehensive global structures as possible.

Although the networking of a global civil society so far rests on a weak and insecure foundation, an increasingly internationally linked movement of Non-Governmental-Organisations work from a global point of view when they deal with human rights, ecology, indigenous knowledge, social relief endeavours, social and economic justice issues. They constitute an effective pressure group in individual areas of politics. They form the organisational core of a global civil society with a vision of a global citizenship.

Today, "globalisation from below", to use professor Richard Falk's term, is proceeding faster than one would have thought a few years ago[16]. Many of the same kind af ideas about the local and the global erupt all over the world. Local citizens' movements and alternative institutions are appearing to meet basic economic needs, to preserve local traditions, to establish ecological chains, to struggle for human rights and dignity. More and more people are crafting their own strategies for survival and development, and in the process are spinning their own transnational webs to connect people across the world.

People's participation in the economic, social, political, and cultural transformation of the World is the central issue of our time. This can be achieved only through adult learning: of the people for the people and by the people.

Notes:

1. Yoshio Katagiri: *"Japanese Education in the Development of Economics"*. In *The Bulletin of Aichi University of Education*. Vol. XXXVV. Kariya, Japan, 1991
2. Lisbon Group: *Limits of competition. Towards a new world contract*. Paris, 1995
3. T.H. Marchall: *"Citizenship and Social Class"* in his *Sociology at the Cross Roads*, Heinemann, London 1963, (original 1950)
4. Maurice Roche: *Rethinking Citizenship. Welfare, Ideology and Change in Modern Society*. Polity Press 1992
5. Maurice Roche: *Rethinking Citizenship. Welfare, Ideology and Change in Modern Society*. Polity Press 1992
6. Shirly Walters and Linzi Manicom (ed.): *Gender in Popular Education*. CACE Publication, Zed Books, 1996
7. Shirly Walters and Linzi Manicom (ed.): *Gender in Popular Education*. CACE Publication, Zed Books, 1996
8. P. Bélanger and H. Mobarak: *"UNESCO and Adult Education"* in *The International Encyclopedia of Education*. Pergamon Press, Oxford
9. Shirley Walters (ed.): *Globalization – Rethinking Adult Education and Training: Impacts and Issues*. ZED Books 1997
10. Michael R. Welton: *"The Bitter Politics of Canadian Adult Education"*. In *Journal of World Education*, 2/1995
11. *Our Creative Diversity. Report of the World Commission on Culture and Development*. UNESCO Publishing 1995
12. Ove Korsgaard: *"Civil Society and World Education"* in *Journal of World Education* 2/1996; Ove Korsgaard: *Kampen om lyset. Dansk voksenoplysning gennem 500 år*. Gyldendal 1997
13. Ove Korsgaard: *"Adult Education, Democracy and Globalisation"*. In *Journal of World Education* 2/1995.
14. Anthony Giddens: *The Transformation of Intimacy*. Polity Press, Cambridge 1992
15. World Assembly Edition, *Citizens Strengthening Global Civil Society*. CIVICUS, Washington 1994
16. Richard Falk: *"The Infancy of Global Civil Society"*. In Lundestad and Westad: *Beyond the Cold War: New Dimensions in International Relations*. Oslo 1992

Adult learning: The Key to the Twenty-First Century

AWE statement about Theme One edited by Dani W. Nabudere:

1.0 Adult Learning

1.1 As we close the twentieth century, adult learning has increasingly become the key concept as a basic right and an important tool for the pursuit of a better life and better world for all in the twenty-first century. As we approach the new century, we have to come to appreciate that adult learning goes beyond the pursuit of literacy and "post literacy" as such.

1.2 We now see adult learning as a life-long process which comprises the right of all people to question and analyse situations around them and afar; the right to imagine and create wider horizons for the human mind; the right to read one's own world and to write one's own history and that of his/her community; the right to have access to educational resources available in one's country and community; the right to develop individual and collective skills in democratic decision making and good citizenship; as well as the right to have and develop one's inner life and identity based on one's cultural heritage and global inter cultural communication.

1.3 Adult learning therefore must include the right to learn to learn, the right to learn to do, as well as the right learn to live together in one world. It means learning to be an active agent in a democracy and the goal is to learn to think, feel, and act democratically. Adult learning must be an integral part of every day life involving political, social, cultural, economic processes involving civil society, the state, and the market.

1.4 For this reason, adult learning should draw on all human cultural resources available to the communities and should include the development and cultivation of systems of indigenous knowledge as well as utilisation of traditional forms and tools af adult learning of the indigenous and traditional communities. The recognition of the rights of these communities to their knowledge and value-systems will enable us also to learn to understand these systems' knowledge and traditional forms of learning for the benefit of the whole of human kind.

2.0 Democracy

2.1 In this context our understanding of democracy will call for a new commitment to deepen its meaning. This will require a reevaluation of the concept itself and its practice. It will also mean a self-understanding of the transformative potential which exist in all our societies to rediscover and reinvigorate the basic human rights as an on-going human process of real life.

2.2 The increasing globalisation processes which are taking place are also leading to the weakening of the nation states. There is a corresponding change in the way people view the existing political structures of power such as political parties, the bureaucracy, the security organs and the way governments are formed and reformed. The distinctive ideological lines which used to exist between the political parties and individuals are now becoming blurred or difficult to discern. In some countries, regional and ethnic differentiation and tensions are reappearing at the very same time as regional economic blocks and regional integrative mechanisms are being worked out to bring together states and economic and social interests.

2.3 All these developments call for renewed attempts at redefining democracy and how it is to be practised in groups, nations and at a global level. All these developments mean that we shall have to rethink the way we look at democracy. Such a new conception will see democracy as something which goes beyond the mere right to vote and be elected, or the right of the majority to make decisions which may affect minority groups adversely, or worse marginalize and oppress them.

2.4 Democracy should have a wider meaning of recognising the rights of individual men and women, minorities and communities to run their own affairs as well as the right of communities to organise their own economies and social life in a sustainable and holistic manner.

2.5 Democracy cannot exist if there is a wide gap between the rich and the poor who in most cases are women. Democracy also means equal relations and opportunities for all. Democracy is a search of the good quality of life. Societies which are poor cultivate a permanent violent climate.

2.6 Therefore the decentralisation of power to local levels has to be linked to the provision of financial and other resources by the Central authorities in order that the community level people have the resources and the support from the central budgets, otherwise the rich will continue to concentrate resources at the Centre at the expense of the poor people in isolated communities.

3.0 Human Rights and Gender

3.1 A new concept of basic human rights should be widened to include the rights of minorities (including ethnic minorities), children, disadvantaged, isolated, and marginalised groups and communities to a better world in which their right to determine their own future is assured. This also means that decisions affecting peoples' lives should as much as possible be made by the affected groups themselves and this will help to decentralise political and economic power which will have a beneficial effect of making life more sustainable economically and ecologically.

3.2 Adult education should promote harmonious gender relations in all societies so that women have equal opportunities in life. The patriarchal model of gender roles encourages unfair and oppressive relations between men and women. Men have the power and women have to submit to that power. An equitable relationship between the sexes requires that women have the opportunity to participate at economic, social, and cultural levels.

4.0 The Local and the Global

4.1 Adult learning should enable communities to "Think locally and act globally" and at the same time enable them to "Think globally and act locally". This will make it possible for communities to learn about real life issues which arise from both the local and the global existence. All this will be necessitated by the very process of economic globalisation which continue to assume greater proportions. Globalisation is pressuring all communities towards a new global consciousness which is partly being influenced by the existence of a risk society in which manufactured uncertainty threatens the existence of the entire human society.

4.2 To cope with the old and new risks, uncertainties and problems created by internationalisation of conflicts and ecological disasters caused in part by the cold war, economic activity and, now, by globalisation of economic life, adult learning should assist individuals and communities across the globe to strengthen common human bonds and human spirit which will enable them to increase human solidarity and cooperation amongst themselves at all levels: the local, the national and the global.

4.3 The mere increase in knowledge to cope with the demands of shifts in patterns of employment and exploding knowledge brought about by globalisation will not in itself bring about human well-being. Only when knowledge is expanded in the way we have described as to how adult learning should be approached in the 21st century (see the first section above) will a sustainable community life be assured both locally and globally.

4.4 The exploding of knowledge means it should be made relevant to the needs and aspirations of billions of poor and disadvantaged communities, groups and individuals. It should be used to improve their livelihood and quality of life and also increase communication and the crisscross flow of information between communities, groups and individuals locally and globally. This will improve their awareness of the world around them and their quality of life.

5.0 Civil Society and Good Citizenship

5.1 The condition for having a learning society is the existence of an active civil society. Civil societies will become increasingly accountable and their actions will become more transparent if it is democratic in its practices in tackling the problems which exist both at the local and the global levels. Such problems are already being addressed on a smaller scale by non governmental organisations. But even here NGOs will have to learn to increasingly empower individuals and communities to assume greater responsibilities for their own lives through their own actions.

5.2 These non-governmental organisations will continue to play an important role, but to be effective they will have to be independent and act as "schools of democracy". They will have to encourage the development of new forms of democracy to enable individuals and communities to have a critical attitude to all issues as well as enabling them to develop the capacity of articulating their concerns in an open way and to be able to challenge those in power to act in a more transparent manner. They should assist individuals to turn "private issues" of public concern into "public issues".

5.3 In this way the NGOs will play an important role in developing local and global solidarity among peoples of the world. They should not restrict their activities in the cultural, relief or "income generating activities" alone, but develop the "third sector" which will enable them to take on political, social and economic issues affecting the local and the global communities in a much more open way. They should also explore and engage the population in entrepreneurial activities which can alleviate the poverty of communities and assist them to become aware of the need to move forwards addressing the wider issues of the need to create sustainable economies and ecologies.

5.4 This implies the emergence of a global civic culture in which local communities assume greater responsibility not only for their own existence but also for the globe/earth. Non governmental organisations through adult learning should address this understanding of the need for an increased global interdependence of communities, groups and individuals within their national borders because such problems arise from the global facts of life, communities groups and individuals will find that these responsibilities actually fall on them if they have to survive, and this will lead to the emergence of global citizenship and a global civic culture.

6.0 Culture of Peace

6.1 The twenty first century should be a century of peace. The cultivation of a global citizenship and culture in which local communities, groups, and individuals assume greater responsibility for their own public affairs will entail the emergence of a culture of peace.

6.2 Peace should not mean the mere absence of war and armed conflict. This is negative peace. We have to move to a situation where peace means the involvement of individuals and communities in the creation of better condition of existence for all and this will minimise the conditions which lead to violent conflicts, for as we have already pointed out above, the existence of poverty creates conditions for the existence of permanent violent environment. This means creating social and economic security for all through human solidarities cooperation and action on local and global scales. This is the positive peace which will eliminate the conditions which lead to negative peace.

6.3 Our children should be brought up in conditions in which their livelihood is secure. We have to remove social and economic relationships which lead to destruction of our natural and human resources. Resources should be equitably distributed and used both on local and global scales. The market alone can not achieve this. There is the wider problem of how cooperating communities can create sustainable economies and societies and this requires human approach in conditions of new approaches to adult learning.

6.4 This requires communities, groups and individuals to think out new ideas which can enable us to utilise the world's resources in a more holistic and sustainable manner, beginning with the reduction of the use of exhaustible resources of energy, (especially through resources to renewable energy resources such as the use of solar energy). This requires a community and individual commitment to reduce energy consumption and move towards new forms of energy use. As we move towards the use of renewable forms of energy, we shall also move towards the use of local resources, and this process will result in greater decentralisation of economic and political life and lead to greater self reliance.

6.5 Thus the creation of a holistic sustainable economic life will enable us to move towards the achievement of sustainable communities on a more democratic basis. This will be the condition for the existence of a culture of peace. Adult learning will help individuals and communities to be involved in active peace building processes, both preventive and "therapeutic". Peace education and peace politics are complementary and the pursuance of both will lead to peace building which has to be done at all levels of society: both at the micro and the macro-levels.

6.6 Peace building and not peace making should be the key concept for the twenty first century. Active peace building can be compared with the use of our common human energies in a positive way. It's a possibility for the ordinary people to develop a peaceful behaviour and this requires a culture of democratic tolerance. Peaceful behaviour is power of the powerless.

6.7 To create conditions for a culture of peace, it will be necessary to create new self-supporting communities existing side by side with urban communities or non-geographical communities based on social interests which cut across national and territorial borders and stations of work.

6.8 The twenty first century will have to develop a balance between unity and diversity which enables individuals and communities to make choices and at the same time accommodate a divergent view points in condition in which common bonds can also exist. This requires the building of non-oppressive and noncohesive horizontal structures rather than authoritarian hierarchical ones. Adult learning will play a leading role in the creation of these new structures which are prerequisite for the existence of cultural peace.

The Authors

Eichberg, Henning

Henning Eichberg was born in Silesia (Germany) and received his academic degrees in sociology and history in Bochum and Stuttgart (Germany). He has held professorships in Odense and Copenhagen (Denmark) and lectured at Austrian, Finnish and French universities. His main fields are studies in body culture and sports, ethnic minorities and national identity. Presently researching at Idrætsforsk., Research Institute of Sport, Body and Culture in Gerlev, Denmark.
Henning Eichberg has written a number of books, several are translated into other languages.

Hansen, Holger Bernt

Holger Bernt Hansen graduated from the University of Copenhagen in 1964 with a masters degree in theology. 1964-67 he held a research fellowship in the Department of Religious Studies at the Makere University, Uganda. At the University of Copenhagen he has held positions in various departments, since 1992 as professor of Church History and African Studies and director of the Centre of African Studies. He has been a member of the Board of Danida since 1987 and its chairman since 1996. His fields of research have included religion and politics in Africa, Ugandan politics and democratization, ethnicity and military rule, Grundtvig's educational ideas and their transfer to the Third World countries. He wrote his doctoral thesis on "Mission, Church and State in a Colonial Setting. Uganda 1890-1925" (London 1984).

Jeria, Jorge

Jorge Jeria is an associate professor of adult education at the Northern Illinois University in De Kalb, Illinois, the United States. He was born in Chile where he received a degree in History and Social Sciences from the Catholic University of Valparaiso. During the agrarian reform programme in Chile he worked with a literacy program in the central region of the country. After the 1973 coup d'état he had to abandon Chile and settled in the United States with his wife Gilda. He completed his Ph. D. at Iowa State University and became an assistant director for minority affairs and professor of international education at that university. In 1988 he became professor of adult education at the Northern Illinois University. In conjunction with his teaching, researcht and publication, he has helped develop a program of adult education in Chile. He is also actively involved with CEEAAL and other adult educational organizations in Latin America and in North America. Further he has been involved with education for demobilization in El Salvador after the signing of the peace treaty. He is currently working in an investigation about the responses of local community to the educational reform in Chile and Brazil.

Kabir, Mabud Fatema

Mrs. Mabud Fatema Kabir has for many years taken active part in different kinds of work to improve the situation for the downtrodden people of Bangladesh, especially the women. She was a member of Parliament and for a short period Deputy Minister of Health andt Population Control. However, she left politics as she felt it was more important to work within the field of education in order to influence a change of attitudes. Mrs. Mabud Fatema Kabir has been director of the Bangladesh Association for Community Education. She has worked in UNICEF and as a consultant to UNDP/UNESCO and holds the position as board member of various NGOs in Bangladesh working within the field of human resource development. Mabud Fatema Kabir is now the managing director of a large contracting firm in Dakar.

Korsgaard, Ove, President AWE

Ove Korsgaard is a researcher at the Royal Danish School of Educational Studies. For more than twenty years he has been active in the Danish Folk High School, as a teacher 1970-74, as principal at Gerlev Idrætshøjskole 1974-91, and as principal at the "free" Teacher's Training College, Ollerup 1991-93. He was chairman of the Association for Folk High Schools in Denmark 1985-91. From 1979 Ove Korsgaard has also worked as a researcher, since 1993 full time. His main fields are studies in body culture and adult education. He has published a number of books, e. g. Fighting about the Body. The Danish History of Body Culture through 200 Years. Gyldendal 1982. Fighting about the Light. The Danish History of Adult Education through 500 Years. Gyldendal 1997. Ove Korsgaard is vice-chairman of a national television station, TV2 Denmark. He is also a member of the Consultative Committee established by UNESCO in connection with the Fifth International Conference about Adult Education in Hamburg 1997.

Nabudere, Dani W., Vice President AWE

Dani W. Nabudere qualified as a lawyer from the Lincoln's Inn in London.

Until he was imprisoned he practised as a lawyer for some years in Uganda. During the period of the transitional government after the Amin regime he was the Ugandan Minister of Culture. When Obote came into power, Dani W. Nabudere had to flee to Tanzania where, for several years, he held a professorship in law at the University of Dar es Salaam. In 1983 he came to Denmark and became a highly esteemed teacher at the International People's College in Helsingør (Elsinore) Denmark, where he worked for eight years. When, at last, it was possible for Dani W. Nabudere to return to Uganda he did not hesitate. He was soon elected to be the representative of his home district to the Constitutional Committee. At the same time he is initiating a school project in his hometown: Yiga Ng' Okola (Learn as you work) – a school for orphans. He has written a number of books, several are used at African Universities. His closest family live in Zimbabwe where his wife works as a teacher.

Petersen, Hanne

Hanne Petersen is professor of law and legal sociology at Ilisimatusarfik, University ot Greenland since September 1995. She is on leave from a professorship in labour law at the University of Copenhagen where she wrote her doctoral thesis on Informal Law in 1992. From 1993-94 she was a Jean Monnet Fellow at the European University Institute in Florence, where she wrote a manuscript for a book entitled "Home Knitted Law. Norms and Values in Gendered Rule Making" (Dartmouth 1996). She has been doing research and been involved in work concerning women's law in a Nordic, European and African context. Further she has been involved in research concerning polycentric law. Her present work deals with legal pluralism especially related to indigenous peoples, and with teaching of especially administrative law in a home ruled indigenous society.

Rónai, Judit, Vice President AWE

Judit Rónai was born in Sopron, Hungary. She studied arts at the Janus Pannonius University of Arts and Sciences, Pécs, Hungary and at the Lorand Eötvös University of Arts and Sciences, Budapest, Hungary. Judit Rónai worked as a teacher at a secondary school from 1981-86, and at a college from 1986-94. In 1988 she founded the Central-European Folk Academy (the Lázló Németh Central-European Folk Academy) Sopron, and became its director. Further she is the founder and president of the Central-European Folk Academy Association and vice president of the Board of Trustees of the Foundation of the Academy.

Torre, Edicio dela, Vice Precident AWE

Edicio dela Torre was born in the Philippines. He was ordained priest in 1968 and left the church in 1987. He worked with farmers' organisations for agrarian reforms and with poor urban organisations for land and housing rights. He also mobilized college students and church people to support the people's struggle. When martial law was imposed he evaded arrest for two years and was part of the leadership of the resistance movement. He was arrested in 1974 and in 1982, and he spent more than nine years in prison. After his release in 1986 he helped establish various NGOs and coalitions, including the Institute for Popular Democracy and Popular Education for People's Empowerment. Edicio dela Torre is the founding chairperson of the Education for Life Foundation ELF which runs the Philippine-Danish Folk School. He is also chairperson of a coalition – Partnership for Agrarian Reform and Rural Development Services.

Walters, Shirley

Shirley Walters lives on the slopes of the Table Mountain in Cape Town, South Africa. She has been active in a wide range of cultural, educational, and women's organisations over the last twenty years. She is the founding director of the Centre for Adult and Continuing Education (CACE) at the University of Western Cape. She has worked as a school teacher, industrial trainer, community educator, researcher and academic. She is currently deeply involved in the reconstruction of a democratic adult educational system in South Africa. Recently she has edited two collections co-published by Zed Books and CACE, "Gender in Popular Education. Methods for Empowerment" with Linzi Manicim, 1996, and Globalisation, adult education and training: Impacts and issues" 1997.

Welton, Michael R

Michael R. Welton received his MA in Anthropology and his Ph. D. in Educational Studies from the University of British Columbia. He is currently professor of adult education at the Mount Vincent university Halifax, Nova Scotia. He has published four book, his most recent being: In Defence of the Lifeworld: Critical Perspectives on Adult Learning (1995). Michael Welton's interests include the history and social theory of adult learning. Currently he is focusing his social theoretical work on developing a conceptual and research framework to study the role of adult educators in maintaining a vital civil society.

The Association for World Education

The Association for World Education is an international, non-governmental, voluntary organisation of individuals and institutions who believe that learning about ourselves and our communities is most effective and satisfying when education reflects an awareness of our intimate relationship to the world as a whole.

OUR STRATEGY

- to promote intercommunication and interaction among individuals and institutions which are working to comprehend and to spread awareness of the global aspects of education.

- to faciliate the exchange and the transfer of ideas, knowledge and experience among such individuals and institutions.

- to spotlight those innovations in education and in development which strengthen the linkages between the local and the global.

- to encourage research and leadership training related to world education.

- to stress the special contribution of a voluntary, people's organisation in working towards the above goals.

OUR VISION

The global society "was the vision of the Association for World Education" when it was first established in 1970. Since then the concept global has been a keyword in our trying to understand the world today.

The word global is connected to the word local. The global and the local are mutually deeply connected which is expressed in the slogans: "Think global – act local!" and "Act global – think local".

Today, the global and the local are inter-connected and interdependent in ways that humanity has not experienced before. Today, the many different local communities around the world share a common destiny. Today, humanity is a geo-ecological entirety within the same biosphere.

The word global is also connected to a concept of one earth, one world, one planet. We live on a globe which has limits. This way of understanding the world is completely new.

This understanding will, in time, place the globe in a new form of togetherness. It will not extinguish the conflict between rich and poor but define it in a new way based on the global limit as a common denominator.

Our Board

President:
Ove Korsgaard
Valorevej 59, 4130 Viby, Denmark

Vice Presidents:

J. Richard Gilliland
P.O. Box 3777
Omaha, NE 68103-0777, USA

Dani W. Nabudere
P.O. Box 403, Mbale, Uganda

Judit Ronai
Szt. Gyorgy U.13, 9400 Sopron, Hungary

Edicio dela Torre
100 Small Horseshoe Drive
Horseshoe Village
Quezon City, Philippines

International Coordinator

Inger Højlund
Avlsmosevenget 12,
4330 Hvalsø, Denmark
Tel.: +45 46 49 22 04   Fax: +45 46 49 95 16